The Goldfish Went on Vacation

the goldfish went on vacation

A MEMOIR OF LOSS

(and Learning to Tell the Truth about It)

PATTY DANN

Afterword by Sallie Sanborn

TRUMPETER

BOSTON & LONDON

2007

Author's Note

In many instances names of people in this book have been changed. In some cases a person is a combination of people I have met.

Trumpeter Books
an imprint of Shambhala Publications, Inc.
Horticultural Hall
300 Massachusetts Avenue
Boston, Massachusetts 02115
www.shambhala.com

9 8 7 6 5 4 3 2 1

First Edition
Printed in the United States of America

♻ This edition is printed on acid-free paper that meets the American National Standards Institute Z39.48 Standard.

Distributed in the United States by Random House, Inc., and in Canada by Random House of Canada Ltd

Library of Congress Cataloging-in-Publication Data
Dann, Patty.
The goldfish went on vacation: a memoir of loss (and learning to tell the truth about it) / Patty Dann; afterword by Sallie Sanborn.—1st ed.
p. cm.
ISBN-13: 978-1-59030-428-0 (acid-free paper)
1. Dann, Patty. 2. Authors, American—20th century—Biography. I. Title.
PS3554.A575Z46 2007
813'.54—dc22
[B]
2006029779

for Jake

ACKNOWLEDGMENTS

To Sallie Sanborn. This book was possible because of her light and wisdom.

To Malaga Baldi, my agent, who always quietly knows what to do.

To Jennifer Brown, my editor. Working with her was a remarkable dance.

To Charles Salzberg, who, as he is with so many books, was the man behind the scene.

To Robert Strohmeier, who has been there for us through all of these years.

And for my students, past and present, who really are my teachers.

The Goldfish Went on Vacation

A Beginning

The snowy night I met Willem at a synagogue in New York City, in February of 1990, I knew we would marry, but I did not know it would last only ten years. He was sitting in front of me and I fell in love with the back of his neck. The floor sloped down to the front, so I didn't realize he was six feet three inches—more than a foot taller than I. He was from Holland, the son of a Mennonite minister, and was drawn to Judaism. I was the child of suburban assimilated Jews. He was almost forty and had never wed, and I was thirty-seven and had just about given up on men, Jewish or otherwise.

Soon after, he dragged me to the Lower East Side, where we met an old rabbi, who looked at us a bit askance and said wisely, "You will have a sweet and crazy life together," which we did.

Nine years later, on an April day in 1999, our little family—Willem; Jake, our three-year-old son, whom we'd adopted from Lithuania as a baby; and I—visited a friend's sheep farm in Connecticut. When we returned to New York, Willem parked the car on the street near our apartment. We walked from the car with Jake riding on Willem's shoulders.

In the middle of the block I said, "Should we get the car seat?"

Willem said, "What's a car seat?" and with that seemingly simple question we entered a new kingdom. Suddenly the work I'd been doing the past twenty years, teaching writing workshops where I give simple memory assignments to help my students, who are all older than fifty, to write their life stories, became my own personal quest to remember my life, my husband's life, the life of our little family before it was lost. I began to do the assignments I gave my students, so that I had a taste of my own medicine, or, as the Dutch would say, "a taste of my own cookie dough."

part one

A Paper Clip

In the three days after our trip to the sheep farm Willem's personality began to change. He always had a bit of a temper, but one morning he asked if I had an "ink pen." He sometimes used different forms of English words, but when I handed him a ballpoint pen, because we didn't own ink pens anymore, he began to scream at me.

He agreed to go to a marriage counselor, who advised Willem to have a checkup. I sat with a furrowed brow in the examining room as the doctor took all of his vital signs. Willem was a marathon runner, in top condition, with healthy lungs and a healthy heart, and everything looked normal, but then the internist began to ask him questions.

The doctor held up a paper clip, and Willem said, "I know what it does, but I don't know the word for it."

English was not Willem's first language, but this was something else.

"I'm concerned. I'm scheduling a brain MRI," said the doctor quietly. "Immediately."

I dropped Willem at his appointment five blocks away and went to pick up Jake at preschool.

Before Willem got home, the phone rang. It was our doctor, who said softly, "I am sorry, but I have very bad news. Your husband has glioblastoma, which is the worst form of brain cancer."

Jake had opened the refrigerator and was pouring orange juice on the floor.

"Do you want me to tell him?" asked the doctor.

Jake was tugging on my sleeve to show me his handiwork.

"No, no thank you," I murmured. "I'll tell him. Tell me one thing. Is he going to die?"

"Yes," he said.

I'm not sure if I said "thank you," but that was the end of that conversation. I did not let myself feel any emotions. For some reason that to this day isn't clear to me, I sneaked into the hall closet, away from Jake, and called our pediatrician.

"I was just told Willem is going to die from brain cancer," I said as evenly as I could. "I don't know what to tell Jake."

"I'm so, so sorry," he said. "Call Sallie Sanborn. I worked with her at Bellevue. If anyone knows this stuff, she does."

In the middle of the night, while Willem and Jake slept, I got up and googled glioblastoma. I read to myself, "The patient will slowly lose all memory, as well as all bodily movement." I had a fleeting image of trying to push Willem in a wheelchair and Jake in his stroller and decided to give Jake's stroller to a pregnant friend. I knew I could not push my husband and my son at the same time.

Flowers

The next day, after our internist had told me Willem had glioblastoma, and after I said I would give my husband the news, I found Willem reading on the couch in the living room. He was rereading a novel by the Dutch author Bernlef called *Out of Mind*. He had given the English version to me for our first anniversary. It is about a couple in which the husband slowly loses his mind and the ability to speak.

I huddled next to him. "Why are you reading this now?" I said.

He shrugged. "Maybe it will help me. I'm having trouble with words."

"Yes," I said, and took a deep breath. "Do you want to know about the MRI?"

"What's that?" he said.

"The picture, the picture they took of your brain."

"Yes, thank you," he said. He had always been a formal man, but already his speech was different.

And then, as simply as I would say we needed a new rug, I said, "You have a brain tumor."

He nodded, and then went back to his book.

A half hour later, Willem called to me while I was in the kitchen trying to feed Jake pasta wagon wheels without weeping.

"What's it called, the tumor?"

I called back as cheerily as I could, "Glioblastoma," trying to make it sound like a lovely flower.

Willem's first surgery lasted four hours. I corrected students' papers as I sat in the over-air-conditioned waiting room. The surgeon came out, and I stood before him waiting to hear our destiny. "We got most of it out," he said.

I stood hugging myself and asked, "When is he going to die?"

"One year, maybe two," he said. Then he said quietly, "Very few people ask that question."

I don't know why I was so blunt. Of course there are miracles. Of course there are exceptions. Breakthroughs are made all the time, but I wanted to know the worst-case scenario. That made me feel more in control, even though I was acutely aware I was in control of nothing.

When I got home from the hospital, Jake was there with his babysitter, racing around the house and wanting to jump on his father as he always did. That night, as I put him to bed, he cried, "I hate Daddy sick. I miss my tall Daddy." Then he sighed and said, "Maybe the sun will come down from heaven and take the disease out of Daddy and give it to the rain and the clouds and he'll be all better."

Summer Camp

When I was ten years old, I went to Camp Whippoorwill, a camp in the Adirondacks that consisted mainly of Jewish girls and Christian counselors, with a similarly populated boys' camp situated neatly across the icy lake. I watched the conductor hoist my heavy trunk onto the northbound train at Croton-Harmon station and then let him pull me up into the car. I knew nobody else on the train or at the camp, and that night I slept in a cabin under the pines with five other girls.

I had trouble falling asleep, listening to the sound of the trees swaying in the wind, but finally I must have, because I woke up at 3:00 a.m. hearing the sobs of the girl in the bunk above me.

"Are you okay?" I whispered.

"No," she sobbed.

I pulled myself up to her bunk. We didn't turn on our flashlights for fear of the counselor's wrath, but we spoke in the dark. I wasn't even sure which girl it was.

It turned out her name was Jane. She is one of my closest friends today. Our children are friends.

That night, as she wept, she said, "I miss some-body."

"That's okay," I said, in an attempt to soothe her. "We're all homesick. Do you miss your mother?"

"Yes," she sobbed.

"Well," I reasoned, "you'll see her on visiting day. That's in four weeks."

"No," she whispered, "I'll never see her again."

She told me her mother had died. (It was years later that I learned it was from a disease called sclero-derma, a cruel disease of the connective tissue. In the wisdom of the day, Jane had been told nothing.)

This is what Jane told me that night, as we clung together on the top bunk. She remembered her mother playing the piano. She remembered her mother sitting up in bed when she came home from school one day. She remembered coming home the next day and her mother wasn't there.

"They took her to the Mayo Clinic," said Jane solemnly.

I wanted to make a joke about it, asking if it was a place where they made tuna fish sandwiches, but I refrained.

"And then," said Jane, "my dad gave away all of my mom's things . . . and we moved."

I knew, in my ten-year-old bones, that there must have been a better way to do things. I had no idea I would be in the position to try another way with my own child.

A Tricycle

Now that I had told Willem about his illness, I knew I needed to tell Jake, too. I decided it was time to call Sallie Sanborn for advice and to set up a time for her and Jake to meet. When I got her on the phone I gave way to nervous chatter and, instead of asking how to talk to Jake, I first asked why she was in this line of work.

"I'm not sure," she said. "I'm just always amazed to see how kids can handle things when they're dealt with openly."

I then had the courage to ask, "But what should I tell Jake?"

"Always tell a child who is losing a parent three things," she said. "One, tell them the truth about what is happening to the parent. Two, if the parent has a disease, name the disease. Three, tell them the doctors are doing everything possible and that they are going to give the parent the best medicine available."

When I hung up the phone with Sallie I went to Jake's room. I sat down on the floor with him, took a deep breath, and said, "Jake, Daddy has a disease in his brain. It's called a tumor."

Jake nodded and said "tubor," and we began to talk a new language, the language of illness, the language of dying, the language of living with it all. I realized that if Jake could learn the words *Tyrannosaurus rex*, he could learn *glioblastoma*.

The day of Jake's first appointment with Sallie, I left Willem resting at home. Jake rode his tricycle fifteen blocks with his sturdy three-year-old legs, with me racing behind.

Sallie's office is on the ground floor of a brownstone building on West Ninety-fifth Street. When we got there, Sallie, a beautiful, energetic blonde, was parking her pale green motor scooter, which endeared her to Jake forever.

"Come on in," she said, ushering us inside. I had been told she rented her office from a pediatrician, but I was surprised to enter the doctor's waiting room, which was a clutter of antique wooden toys and home to a real sheepdog, who was asleep under a chair. Jake was ready to move in. A welcoming nurse with a heavy Irish brogue greeted us.

Sallie's office is tiny but perfectly organized. Somehow she manages to keep a little sandbox on the floor, stuffed animals snuggled in the corners, books, a real doctor's kit complete with real syringes, a fleet of rescue vehicles, dolls, board games, and a stash of balloons for popping or filling with water, all comfortably within reach.

I sat with Jake that first day as they played together.

"I hate sick," said Jake.

Sallie handed him a stuffed dog, and he spent a lot of time intently bandaging one of the dog's legs.

As Sallie and Jake played, I sat on the floor in the corner watching them. We all would die, we all will die. Why should this be so difficult to talk about?

"I want to play cars," Jake announced, and he began to make a complicated jumble of a traffic jam with tiny matchbox cars all over Sallie's floor. Jake always had a passion for cars. His first sentence was, "I want cars."

Jake sat there crashing the cars together.

"It's hard when things don't go the way we want," said Sallie, as Jake smashed a toy ambulance into a tow truck.

"Call me any time," she said as we left. "It will be a bit of a roller coaster ride."

A Baseball Game

"Live in the moment."

"All you have is the day."

"We're all terminal."

These phrases ricocheted through my head. Some friends immediately looked up Willem's illness and forwarded their dire discoveries to me. Others told me it must be because he used a cell phone, even though he did not own one. "Blueberries," wrote a friend on a postcard from California. "The antioxidants will do it. Blueberries are the key."

Willem was a historian. He worked as the director of a photo archive at an international relief agency and had spent so long on his doctoral dissertation that I called him Dr. Footnote. And though he was a researcher, he never once looked up his disease and had no desire to join any kind of support group. He wanted to return to his job and work with his beloved photographs and papers, he wanted to write a book about displaced persons in World War II, he wanted to go to Prague for his fiftieth birthday, he wanted to take Jake and me bike riding in Belgium and run a marathon someday in Tokyo.

"I have no interest in cancer," he declared, "even if it has an interest in me."

Yet he knew what the outcome of his illness would be. It was his idea to call the cemetery where my grandparents are buried.

A woman calmly quoted prices over the phone. "Do you want a single, double, or triple site?"

When Willem was back on his feet, with a Nike headband covering his scar, and Jake was at preschool showing a squashed penny at show-and-tell, we drove out of the city to the bucolic cemetery on a hillside. I was nervous having Willem drive. I have always been nervous with him at the wheel. He had learned to drive as an adult in this country, because, when growing up in Holland, his mode of transportation was his bicycle. Now he loved "to put the pedal to the metal" and scream Dutch words of joy as he accelerated.

We arrived safely at the cemetery, and a gentle man listening to a Mets/Cardinals game on a transistor radio held to his ear showed us around.

"Now do you want to be buried foot to foot or head to head?" he asked, taking the radio from his ear for the briefest possible moment and pointing out where other members of my family lay.

After we mumbled something about "head to head" we took the proper papers to fill out, and my head spun wondering when my time would be. Afterward we went out for cheeseburgers and milk shakes, then drove back to the city, went home, and made love.

An Airplane

had wanted a baby since I was eight years old. Sometimes it was tiny whispers behind my ears, and sometimes it was a longing like a wound, but I turned thirty-nine and still I was not with child.

People said to Willem and me, "Go on vacation."

To me they privately said, "Don't eat yogurt." "Don't think about it." "Stop running." "Stop swimming." "Do a handstand afterward."

We tried these things.

The morning I turned forty, I awoke and whispered to Willem, "Let's adopt a baby."

In fact, I had been dreaming of adopting a baby for a long time. When asked on my college applications what I saw myself doing in twenty years, I had written, "I want to have an orphanage and be a photographer. I am very interested in children whose parents have died or otherwise abandoned them." For years I had had dreams of walking into an orphanage and bringing children home.

On the plane to Poland to pick up Jake, I was so excited that I did not read a word or sleep a wink. We touched down early in the morning on May 20, 1996, in a misty rain. I was now forty-two years old. Willem was almost forty-five. We had a three-hour layover at the airport before we were to fly Lithuanian Airlines to Vilnius. We made our way to the cafeteria for sausages and scrambled eggs. Cher was singing "It's in His Kiss" over the sound system.

By the time we boarded the Lithuanian airplane, I was having an out-of-body experience. The plane was an old Russian-made military-looking aircraft like I'd only seen in very old black-and-white movies. We boarded the plane in the rear, and I felt like we were entering a cave. I banged the stroller up the steps as if I'd done it a thousand times, while Willem carried our bags.

We touched down in Lithuania at 4:00 p.m. It was one hour later than Polish time, and it was rainy and dark. The arrival terminal looked more like a bus station than an airport. The Lithuanian language sounded like the song of beautiful birds. We took a wild taxi ride, racing to the orphanage, or "children's house," as they called it, to meet our son.

After fifteen minutes we entered the city, which even in the rain I could see was a blend of stark Soviet apartment buildings melded with medieval cobblestones and churches. Tina Turner was pumping out a litany of love on the radio as the driver continued to race through the slick streets. Ten minutes later we were heading out of town again, up a hill with lush trees, and then we made an abrupt turn onto a road with no discernible sign. A few more minutes and we pulled onto the gravel driveway of a low, pale yellow brick building.

We entered the children's house through such a low doorway that Willem had to bend forward to go into the cold, dark hall. We followed the director up two flights of stairs. We could hear the chatter of children and someone talking Lithuanian very loudly on a telephone.

Suddenly a woman appeared wearing a long yellow cotton dress and a bandana on her head.

"Please," she said, pointing to a room off the hallway.

Willem and I stepped into a small room with two worn red couches and a set of shelves that were bare except for a lone Miss Piggy doll. A crucifix was the only ornamentation on the walls. We sat quietly for fifteen minutes waiting for our son.

And then a nurse brought in a startlingly beautiful baby, swaddled in a red outfit, with chubby cheeks and a bright smile. He reached out his arms. I reached for him and cradled my plump son. Willem and I took turns holding him, as the nurse sat on the opposite couch smiling and nodding.

This moment I had waited so long for was like hearing a bell ring a perfect chime. It was not like fireworks. It was a feeling of fullness. "Here you are, little boy," I whispered. "I've been looking all over for you." It was a deep sense of finding someone whom I'd lost for a very long time. We had become a family.

The next morning Willem and I went to a little café that was playing "Yellow Submarine" on the jukebox and ordered coffee. He was used to the strong Dutch kind, and I had my first sip of Lithuanian brew, black with extra sugar.

"Now we're three," said Willem.

Years later, waiting in the hospital Family Room for the brain surgeon to give me his report after Willem's first surgery, I stood hugging myself, and I had a physical memory of holding my son in my arms for the first time. And then when the surgeon said Willem had one year to live, I had the sensation of my baby being taken from my arms. To adopt him we had three letters of recommendation from friends telling in great detail what a lovely couple we were, what a wonderful family we would be.

I felt like I was letting my son down. Now it would be just the two of us.

Calendars

Before the illness, Willem and I led a peculiarly orderly life, though in my mind I'd always felt like I was stepping from slippery rock to slippery rock in a rushing brook. It was no accident I'd married a Mennonite. Dirty dishes were never left in the sink. Thank-you notes were written. The shoes were neatly matched at the front door. Dutch friends and family visited regularly from Holland. Jake had a bath every night. I read to him in English, and then Willem read to him in Dutch.

We took Jake to preschool together. I picked him up. Often Jake and I waited outside our apartment building for Willem to come home from work. In summer I'd sometimes have a cold beer waiting for him. Before we were married I once waited for him at the subway wearing a raincoat and nothing else. After we became parents we had a babysitter one night a week and went out to movies or museums. Other evenings, Willem often went for a run in Central Park. On the weekends, I wrote and swam and cooked. Willem took Jake to museums and methodically tried different playgrounds around the city. Willem always did the laundry.

The nights I taught at the YMCA, Willem stayed with Jake, and I always came home to a very neat house, with Jake asleep. Willem would either be at his desk, where he studied colonial texts with meticulous footnotes while listening to chamber music, or he would be watching a baseball or basketball game, depending on the season.

Calendars were important to both of us. In every Dutch home there is a birthday calendar that often hangs in the bathroom, a perpetual calendar of family and friends. I still have the birthday calendar that came with Willem when he moved in. We always had a kitchen calendar, usually bought at a museum gift shop. Willem had his daily planner he kept in his briefcase, and I had a similar one I kept in my purse. We even had a calendar in Jake's room, recording the big events in his young life.

One evening after the surgery, I returned home from class and found clothes flung all over the floor. The refrigerator door was open. There was a Dutch CD of children's songs playing very loudly, but, remarkably, Jake was sound asleep.

And Willem was at his desk, writing intently. He

stood up and bowed when he saw me, not an uncommon act for him, but when I asked about the mess, he did not respond. I cleaned up the clutter as Willem sat closer to the television screen than usual watching a baseball game.

It was as if there were a stranger in the house. As Willem was watching the game, I wandered over to his desk to see what he was working on. All over the surface were yellow Post-it notes, scribbled on with tiny letters, sentence after skewed sentence in a handwriting I'd never seen before.

Suddenly, in just a week's time, my husband was a different person, and the lovely van Gogh calendar we kept in the kitchen, with the self-portrait of Vincent and his bandaged head, was filled with doctor's appointments.

Candy

In June Willem began radiation, and a battalion of our friends agreed to take turns walking with him to his appointments and back, which would be five days a week for six weeks, except he got off the Fourth of July. On the Fourth of July the radiologists, if not cancer, would take a holiday.

On the weekend of Father's Day, Willem was restless and twice slammed down his books on his desk, which he'd never done before. Jake began kicking his legs under the sheets like a small warrior each night when I tried to get him to sleep.

I called Sallie.

"Children are like small barometers," she said. "They feel every change in the house."

The next morning Willem woke up screaming. He had developed a blood clot. We rushed to the hospital, with Jake in his dog pajamas, carrying far too many toy cars, and waited while it was established that Willem would require daily and nightly injections of blood thinner, either in his thigh or in his stomach.

I knew I would have to learn how to give the injections, but for the first two nights a cheerful man, a visiting nurse named Glenn, arrived at the apartment just as I was trying to wrestle Jake into bed, not an easy task normally.

When Glenn began to unpack his bag and take out a syringe, and Jake stood there clutching a toy cement mixer, I held up my hand to stop Glenn. I found a stray bag of M&M's in the kitchen drawer from the previous Halloween, and I literally threw the M&M's into Jake's room, shut the door after him, and motioned Glenn to take care of Willem in our bedroom. Then I ran in to distract Jake. This was not a moment I was proud of.

The next night Glenn arrived and Jake leaped into his arms.

"This time I suggest another way," said Glenn, and I followed his lead. I figured he spent his life walking into people's homes seeing all kinds of illnesses, night after night, with hundreds of children running around.

"Come," Glenn said to Jake.

He put Jake down and they went hand in hand into the bedroom to see Willem.

Willem waved weakly. "Welcome," he said in his charming Dutch accent. "May I offer you a drink?"

"Another time, thank you," said Glenn. "Right now your son is going to help me give you a shot."

I blanched, but Glenn continued and Willem smiled. Jake stood right next to his father, patting the big scar on his head.

"Put out your hand," said Glenn, "and keep it flat."

Jake obeyed as Glenn opened his bag and took out a syringe. He ripped open the wrapper and laid the sharp syringe on Jake's little hand. Jake didn't move. Then Glenn took the syringe from Jake and told me to take an alcohol wipe from his bag, which I did.

"Open it and hand it to Jake," he said quietly.

I wanted to refuse. This was not part of our bedtime routine. Willem was supposed to read Jake *Curious George* in Dutch.

"Now, Jake," said Glenn as he pulled up Willem's shirt, "wipe this gently on your daddy's stomach."

He steered Jake's hand and they did it together. Then Glenn gave Willem the shot. And so it went. Glenn came three more nights, teaching me how to give the injections, and Jake was there through all of it. Jake was fascinated.

A Notebook

At our second appointment with the neurologist, an elegant young man in a tailored suit, Willem and I sat across from his desk like school-children.

"That's a lovely tie," said Willem.

"Thank you," said the doctor.

And then he proceeded to tell us that Willem might begin to lose the language he learned most recently first. Willem had studied English in school in the Netherlands but only spoke it when he arrived in New York at the age of thirty-five on a Fulbright. I never learned Dutch. I tried, taking lessons from an earnest Dutch graduate student once a week for ten weeks, who insisted I was learning, but at the end of the semester all I knew was how to count to twenty and say five swear words that seemed to require a lot of spit to pronounce.

Jake was chirping away in English and understood Dutch at this point. His first word was "More!" I had a sweet notebook where I had carefully written down Jake's words—"scoobie" for excuse me, "perket" for perfect, "I want to soft the dog," instead of pet the dog, and "all my byself," instead of all by myself. Now the notebook was filled with names and amounts of steroids, charts with precise times for Willem to take the vile stuff, and the names of the drugstores that carried the blood-thinning medication.

Brain cancer was now part of our language. Dutch paled in comparison.

A Boat

cried in the shower every day. I cried walking to
work. I would tell women at the checkout counter
at the supermarket about Willem and weep. I felt
compelled to speak the words to grown-ups, words
I still had a trouble speaking to Jake, even if Sallie
said I should.

Along with the injections, I had to give Willem
steroid pills every three hours. I had to hunt for a
place in the apartment that was high enough so Jake
couldn't get them but low enough so that I could.
Willem used to tease me that I married him because
I needed someone to reach things. Now he was lying
down in bed and I was on my own. I found a high
shelf in the closet outside our bedroom that Jake
could not climb up to but I could reach if I stood on
Jake's high chair. As I was wobbling on the chair in
the dark at 3:00 a.m., trying not to topple over,
trying not to spill the pills, trying not to wake Jake,
trying to keep Willem calm, who was calling for me
to make him hard-boiled eggs, "not too hard, lieveling"
(*lieveling* is Dutch for "darling"), I realized I was becoming a single mother.

The last day of preschool in June, I walked Jake alone, leaving Willem at home in bed. Jake said. "Where's Daddy? Where did he go?"

In the past, the three of us often walked Jake to school, and for the last block Willem carried Jake on his shoulders, a ritual that gave both of them enormous pride, but I wasn't strong enough to carry Jake on my shoulders, and he didn't want me to. That was not my job.

How do you explain to a child of almost four about staples in his father's head, radiation, and chemotherapy? When a child is so used to reading a parent's face and his hand gestures, if he suddenly stops carrying him on his shoulders, bends to pet animals when he never did before, suddenly laughs hysterically watching *Sesame Street* and refuses to watch any sports on TV when he used to sit for hours watching basketball and baseball games with his son on his knee, how do you explain?

I had a picture in my head of those old movies where all the people are on a boat and the audience sees the rushing waterfall ahead but the people in the boat do not.

A Birthday

The main challenge was not to say good-bye to Willem yet, to have each day filled and be thankful, and yet I felt myself being pulled by the hand into the future by my young son. I couldn't help leaping forward to the state of widowhood, of raising a child on my own.

In the orphanage I had turned to Willem and said, "You'll take him to soccer, right?" and he had said, "Of course, lieveling. It will be my pleasure."

Who would teach Jake to shave and tie a tie? Until now the challenge for me in our marriage was to live with a man from another culture, and my failing to learn Dutch had been a disappointment for both of us. Now Sallie was to become the translator, helping to explain what the doctors said to me and helping me to talk to friends and family and Jake.

On June 21 of 1999, a week before Willem's forty-ninth birthday, I asked Jake what we should get for his father.

"A cookie, a pill, and a cake," he said solemnly.

On the day of Willem's birthday, there were many calls from Holland. In Holland people visit you on your birthday. You are the host and are expected to stay home all day, and into the night, serving food and pastries, wine and strong coffee. Another tradition in Holland is to decorate the chair of the "birthday boy or girl," but this year we forgot. People did visit, and I got tears in my eyes as Jake and I put forty-nine candles and one for luck in the cake. Luck and radiation seemed to have equal billing in our home. Jake helped Willem blow out the candles, and they both sang "Are you one? Are you two? Are you three?" up to forty-nine, and they both confused some of the numbers.

Willem was a different person from when he was forty-eight. In some ways he was not the man I married. I think in some ways he would have said I was not the woman he married either. When we met, I thought my role in life was to stand behind the curtain and peer out at the actors as they performed. Now I felt that I'd been asked to be center stage as I gracefully escorted my sweetheart to the River Styx.

part two

A Phone Book

They say a man falls in love with his eyes and a woman falls in love through her ears. As my husband drifted away from me, I turned to my students' stories. For the past twenty years I'd had my socks knocked off by the stories my students wrote and read aloud. I returned to my Tuesday-evening class at the YMCA and listened, as my students read their stories, as if I were listening to a celestial radio; every time I turned the dial I was enchanted.

Karen, a woman with a curved spine but sparkling eyes, read, "My grandparents were both mute and wore high button shoes. They invented their own sign language. They came to this country from Poland when they were fifteen. They were married for seventy years."

Celia, from South Africa, an elegant white journalist left staggered by a stroke, was able to write in almost illegible handwriting. She read, "My father was a carpenter in our hometown outside of Johannesburg. He left raw planks of wood out in the yard to age, and when it rained, the sweet smell of wet cedar filled our house."

Ruth was a refugee from Germany, a slim woman who wore scarves in the most sophisticated way. She had arrived on the island of Manhattan in 1939 with her young husband and nothing else. When they arrived they went to a phone booth, opened the phone book, and picked out a new last name that sounded neither German or Jewish—Larsen. Janine was a beautiful, open-faced black woman who wore her hair tied back in a chignon. She was raised by her aunt, a dwarf who used to sneak her out of school every Friday to go to the Polo Grounds to watch Negro League baseball. Doria was a bubbly Greek American whose mother had warned her of the evils of men and persuaded her to go to pharmaceutical school, believing that only women were pharmacists and so she would not be tempted by sex, only to find out that Doria was one of only two women in the entire school. There was Theresa, first married, then a nun, now a lesbian, and Eloise, from Leominster, Massachusetts, who got in trouble with her Yankee mother for saying "Hi" to a grown-up instead of "Hello, Mrs. Smith."

Hilda, an eighty-year-old student of mine, said, "I stopped lying when I turned seventy." At the time, I was still under fifty and didn't yet know what she meant, but now I was beginning to have a clue. For years, as I preached the necessity of writing boldly and honestly about real life, I could write only fiction. Until real life intervened. These women had survived everything, and their stories were starting to give me the courage to do the same.

Food

On our fifth visit to Sallie I was so weary from getting up every three hours to give Willem steroids, and then get Jake back to sleep after he'd wake upon hearing me rummaging around, that I had confused the time of the appointment and got there early. Jake liked visiting the sheepdog and playing with the wooden trucks so much that he didn't mind when I slid down into a chair and closed my eyes.

I longed to eavesdrop on threads of Sallie's conversations through the wall, but I heard nothing. I have always longed for stories. I've spent my whole life being healed by them, and now the only way I could get Jake to sleep each night without Willem's reading to him in Dutch was to tell him story after story about when he was a fat baby and we met him in Lithuania and bought baby food at a store where they used an abacus instead of a cash register.

It was the same with Willem as well. He would stay up late, agitated by the steroids, and I would remind him of our first married summer in Holland when we played Ping-Pong outside and ate strawberries until the sun went down at 10:00 p.m. And finally, finally, Willem would sleep and I would read my students' stories from around the world.

These stories had a curative effect on me. Though the stories had as much heartache as happiness, they filled me with a kind of inner peace. Each morning I asked Willem to tell me the stories of when he was a little boy growing up in a parsonage in the town of Utingeradeel in the north of Holland. I was starved to hear his stories.

At age four a child remembers being three, even two years old, but those memories leave as we get older. I scribbled down memories of Jake and of Willem like a madwoman, in notebooks, on stray pieces of paper, on the palm of my hand, knowing that within a year Willem's personal history would be forgotten by him. What would be his last word, his last word in the world?

Stamps

One bitter-cold January evening, years before I got married, I arrived to teach my Tuesday 6:00 p.m. class at the YMCA and realized I'd left my notebook with the assignments at home.

My boyfriend and I had split up two months earlier. We had lived together through his medical school and internship. I was confused. I wasn't sleeping or eating much. I had purchased a watch; I had prided myself on never wearing one, but in truth I was always asking my boyfriend the time. When I bought the watch I'd joked to the salesman, "Now nobody has to give me the time of day," and was met with a wan smile.

That cold January I managed to have both milk and eggs on hand at the same time, neither of which had gone bad, but I was still forgetting things. I would leave my wallet at home when I went out. I put my toothbrush in the refrigerator. The class was my anchor, and as I scanned my book bag and saw that the notebook was missing, I panicked, but only for a moment, because these older people always worked their spell on me.

"Okay," I said firmly, "write for ten minutes in class about . . ." and as I spoke I had no idea how the sentence would end until I said, "stamps. Write about a memory of stamps, postcards, envelopes, or the post office."

My students bent their heads to their papers as if in prayer, and I left the room for ten minutes. I stood outside in the bustling YMCA hallway. The guests from the bare-budget hotel rooms, were often scurrying to the swimming pool. The walls were covered with artwork from the day-care center and the preschool. There was the clanging of barbells from the fitness center, and the bulletin board was plastered with notices of AA meetings, Road Runners Club clinics for the New York Marathon, and super masseuses. The whole building smelled of chlorine. This is where Mark Chapman slept the night before he murdered John Lennon.

I sat outside my classroom and thought of stamps. I recalled the first-day issues my brother had collected, and when I could jimmy the lock on his door I would sneak into his private male domain, the room with the brown and white bedspread and baseball pennants on the walls, and lie on his bed and look at the first-day-issue stamps, stuck together from the heat.

Willem collected stamps from the time he was a little boy, as did his grandfather in Holland, who prided himself on carrying his bicycle up six flights of narrow stairs every day. My husband loved stamps. On our honeymoon on the scrubby island of St. Eustatius, which advertised proudly that it had "no sandy beaches," he wrote forty-three postcards to family and friends, carefully positioning colorful stamps in the corner of the cards.

Whenever he received a piece of mail, he studied the stamp to see if it had been canceled. If not, after he read the letter or card or opened the package, he would carefully cut around the stamps and leave them to soak overnight in the sink, to use on other letters. The canceled stamps were carefully cut out as well. They are in an enormous shopping bag for my son.

As I sat outside the classroom at the YMCA on that January evening, I had no idea that someday I would have a husband from Holland or a son from Lithuania who would someday sit sifting through his father's stamps like an archaeologist.

Shoes

was born in New York City in 1953. My parents and older brother and I lived in a small house in a small suburb. It was called a "modern" house then, which meant there was a lot of glass and we had to run hoses on the roof in the summer to keep it cool. When I was three, the age Jake was when Willem got sick, we moved farther from the city to a bigger house next door to a convent, Helpers of the Holy Souls.

The convent was the center of my childhood. The tree-lined grounds were full of nuns in black regalia, wimples, and shined, tightly tied shoes. Every morning at 7:00 a.m. they walked past our mailbox in tidy rows with their heads bent. They carried tiny black prayer books and chanted Latin in unison. What it sounded like they were saying, over and over and over again, was "My mommy and daddy are in fifth grade, my mommy and daddy are in fifth grade."

As the nuns passed I could smell their clean starched robes and polished shoes. I put my hands together in solemn prayer and whispered their prayer with them, "My mommy and daddy are in fifth grade. My mommy and daddy are in fifth grade."

In fact my parents were not. My mother was a reporter on the local newspaper and now had three cockeyed kids to care for. My father was a television executive often in "the city," which is what we called Manhattan, or "out on the coast," which of course was Los Angeles.

My parents are still alive and well. My father had grown up in Detroit, an observant Jew, with an older brother and younger sister and loving parents. One morning, when my father was two years old, he could not get out of bed.

He had polio, and until he was eighteen years old, he wore a heavy, ugly brace on his right leg. I never saw him with the brace but he always wore a different size shoe on that foot. I only knew him as my father wearing a suit and hat, running with an uneven gait for the 7:35 train to New York City every morning. All the men wore suits and hats. On the way home they sat in the smoking car playing cards, drinking, and smoking cigars. The wives picked them up at the train station.

His closet was littered with the shoes that never fit him. When my father was away on the coast or in the city, I'd sneak into his closet and clomp around in those odd shoes in front of the mirror, singing "Somewhere over the Rainbow" in what I called the "odd-shoe dance."

As I thought of life with my father, I tried to imagine Jake's life without his father, and I wondered, when Jake grew up, if he would be able to remember him.

Jungle Gym

At our next meeting with Sallie, as Jake went into her office to make wild traffic jams with tiny cars, Sallie stopped me at the door.

"I want you to watch out for three things," she said.

I rummaged in my bag for a pen and notebook.

"No, no," she said, resting her hand on my arm. "Just listen. There are three things to look out for in kids when their parents are ill," she repeated.

"One: children tend to think they might have caused the illness. (They may ask you over and over if it is their fault.) Two: they're frightened they can catch it (even though you may have reassured them a hundred times that you can't catch cancer). Three: they might get sick because they're worn down or feign illness to get attention, and there's no question kids are more accident-prone when their parents are sick. I see it all the time. Most of their worries will come at bedtime, when the demons come out, as with all of us. With it will come the endless questions, which will appear and reappear, perhaps all of their lives: 'How did this happen? Why did it happen?

Will it happen to me?' Children might experience all of these things, some of these things, or none."

It was true that on the day of Willem's first surgery Jake had indeed flipped over on his tricycle, causing a gushing wound to his forehead. A dear friend of mine, whose husband had pancreatic surgery, has three children, and her middle child fell off the jungle gym the day of his father's surgery.

It was also true that, out of the blue, when Jake was playing Candyland the night before Willem's surgery, he had said he had a headache. He put his small hand to his forehead. "Is this cancer?" he'd asked.

It is truly a luxury to take one's child to a therapist when these things happen, but if one can't, it's important to realize that not talking to children about the illness of a loved one could make things worse.

When a child loses a parent, of course it's good if the child gets angry rather than turning inward, but it's remarkable how adults often don't expect a child to have feelings as intense or for as long a period as an adult.

Sallie got a call from a school guidance counselor about a little boy whose father had died only a month before.

"He's dictatorial, grabbing other kids' toys," said the counselor.

"But his father died only a month ago," said Sallie.

"He did fine at the funeral though," said the counselor, "and I thought he'd moved on."

The boy was three years old.

Tape

When Willem got sick, Jake began bandaging everything in sight. "I need more Band-Aids," he'd insist. He put Band-Aids on all of his toy cars and trucks. One morning when Willem was sound asleep, he put Band-Aids all over our wooden bed frame.

One of Sallie's first patients was named Nathaniel. Nathaniel wasn't dealing with death but with his parents' divorce. He seemed to be handling it all, but one day when he was meeting with Sallie he brought along his lunch bag, which had ripped, and he was so distraught he was weeping. Sallie suggested taping it, an activity not uncommon when children are surrounded by life that is ripped or broken.

"We must have put a roll of tape on that bag. We spent almost an hour taping. He didn't talk much, but we patched that bag together. We couldn't save his parents' marriage, but that bag was saved."

Whispering

I n my early days of teaching, I walked wearily into class and asked my students to write a memory of shoes.

As I sat outside the classroom, I thought of the blue sneakers left in the cubbyhole of Jimmy, my boyfriend in fourth grade. He was from England, and his mother taught horseback riding to children. We attended an Episcopal private school together; I, a Jew among Christians, singing "Onward Christian Soldiers" valiantly each morning at assembly as I stood proudly next to Jimmy. I loved Jimmy. He was the first child I knew who wore eyeglasses, tiny metal frames on his sweet face.

One November morning, after taking the long bus ride to school, I arrived a little early. When I walked into my homeroom class, the principal was whispering to the teacher at the blackboard.

"Jimmy's dead," she said.

All morning in class the teacher didn't mention it. It was only at lunch in the cafeteria that I overheard from another whispering teacher that Jimmy had been killed when he was horseback riding, jumping over a fence. He wasn't wearing a helmet. Jimmy's blue sneakers stayed in his cubbyhole the rest of the year, and when nobody was looking I'd hold the sneakers to my ears and pretend I could hear Jimmy singing to me.

The next November, in 1963, when I was ten years old, I was in social studies class reading the purple-ink mimeographed sheet on checks and balances in the government when the principal again came to our class, this time to whisper that President Kennedy had been killed.

I remember the smell of the ink from the old mimeograph machine, but I also remember the whispering, whispering about Jimmy, whispering about President Kennedy, and both times I felt that somehow I had done something wrong. What could I have done to save my friend? To save the president? These were the only deaths I knew about as a child, and both times, I did not talk to anybody about what had happened that day.

A River

When I was seventeen I went to Bennington College in Bennington, Vermont. I lasted one year. In that school year, there was no president because of a previous scandal; there were about seven eccentric boys and a few hundred wild girls. Kids were shooting up heroin in the bathroom and making love there as well.

Meals were served in the main dining hall except for Sunday evenings, when each house was responsible for their own dinner. I went to the living room of our house the first Sunday night to find a naked girl covered in whipped cream lying on a table. I was not prepared for such things. I took a photography class, and the teacher with the long beard told me we didn't need a camera for photography. I enrolled in an anthropology course with a famous anthropologist and diligently sat in the front row of the tiny classroom where it was held and listened to her talk of the Amazon. At the end of the year, on my comments (we did not get grades), she had written, "It would have been a better year if you had attended class."

I was a virgin, apparently one of the few, if my

colleagues were telling the truth. I met a boy from Kentucky who took my hand one afternoon after biology lab and said, "I've always wanted to fuck a Jewish girl."

After freshman year, I fled west in July. I got in a Volvo, which we were proud of calling a "vulva," with three others who were dropping out. The four of us drove across the country, stopping only to fill up on gas. We'd each drive a tank and then rotate. This was before the fifty-five-miles-per-hour speed limit, and we roared across the plains, making it to Oregon in four days.

Exhausted, we fell out of the car into a farmer's field, stole corn, roasted it on an open fire, and dove into the icy Willamette River.

I ended up enrolling at the University of Oregon, where there were equal numbers of girls and boys and Steve Prefontaine, the runner, was the hero. And I fell in love with Alex, son of an undertaker. Alex wore purple bell-bottoms and had a water bed.

At night, after we made love, he would tell me stories of the times he had spent after school in the funeral parlor.

"We were never lonely as kids," he said. "I felt peaceful there with all the bodies. It was only later I learned people considered it strange. My dad died when I was five, and I think it comforted me to be there, like I was closer to him."

I thought of Alex often during those months after Willem's diagnosis, and wondered if Willem would be at Jake's fifth birthday party.

Kitchen Table or Dining Room Table

I have always longed to be comfortable at a kitchen table or dining room table, but I often feel restless, as if a hummingbird were beating in my chest. I gave the assignment of kitchen table or dining room table to my students to comfort myself.

Janine wrote about the prostitutes who, when she was a child, sat around in their negligees counting their money every morning, cigarettes in their mouths, their silk-stockinged feet propped up on the kitchen table.

Theresa wrote of the quiet table in the convent, where only a slight coughing every so often was heard, the place where she ached to scream out when she got word her mother had died.

Doria wrote of her Greek father, who owned the local coffee shop, where she had every single meal of her childhood at the table near the bathroom. She did her homework at that table, and it's also where she let boys touch her under the table while her father was in the kitchen.

I had one student, Martha, who wore her hair in a gray ponytail tied with yarn. She wrote of coming

59

home from school in her little fishing village in Maine to find her father laid out on the dining room table. He had died while she was at school, and nobody had come to get her.

While I was trying to prepare dinner for my family earlier that night, my husband was vomiting in the bathroom and my child was telling me, "If Daddy doesn't have to have dinner, I don't either." I completely lost my appetite. The possibility of a family table now felt even further away. And when Willem and Jake were finally asleep, I often ate chocolate ice cream standing up at the sink late at night.

Swimming Pool

When I was twenty-nine and scared to turn thirty alone, I woke up on the first hot Saturday in June, got into my car, an old Peugeot, and pointed it north. As soon as I got out of the city I swerved onto back roads. Maps and interstates always baffled me. I was better with signs on two-lane roads.

Somehow I landed in Vermont, and soon after I saw signs for Middlebury, I veered off at a community swimming pool full of shrieking teenagers and children.

I climbed into the backseat and stealthily changed into my bathing suit. After the initial embarrassment of walking from the car to the pool in my flowered two-piece with my towel draped around me, I dove in as if I lived there and swam ten laps, dodging children playing Marco Polo, then pulled myself out and lay on the hot cement to dry off. Then I drove off in my bathing suit, still heading north.

I swam in six public pools on my way up to Montreal, where my best friend, Mary, and her husband lived. Somehow if I could see their faces

I knew I would be okay. I stayed one night in Montreal and spent most of it weeping along with their infant son. Then I turned around and headed home, stopping at all the pools I had hit on the way up. Driving in my bathing suit was a delightful experience, and swimming anonymously in pools, where nobody knew my story and I could imagine theirs, gave me strength.

As Willem's body began to fail him, I swam mile after mile at the YMCA. Their swimming pool features the most beautiful ornate tiles from Spain. People always say, "The tiles are from the king of Spain," as if they were from a fairy tale, but in fact it was the Spanish government that gave them. The pool is surrounded by stained glass windows, and when the sun is shining, it is like swimming in a small cathedral. The pool became my refuge. In the water I felt as if I were strengthening my body to be a mother and father to Jake. Gliding through the water, I felt that the burdens at home were lessened, but, I admit it, some days I would imagine swimming far, far away and never returning home at all.

Sewing

My first day back to teaching after we adopted Jake, I walked into class as if I were wearing high heels for the first time, tottering along and trying desperately to seem in control.

I told my students to write something about sewing, and I went into the ladies' room to look in the mirror, to see if I still existed. I saw a haggard middle-aged woman with a small smudge of banana on her collar.

When I was six years old I took sewing lessons on Thursday afternoons in the attic of Mrs. Bartlett's home, who might have been forty-five, but she was a grandmother, and the house smelled of fresh fabric and cinnamon. Each Thursday my mother picked me up from school and handed me a thermos of coffee milkshake with a raw egg in it. I stood behind her in the backseat of the station wagon, stroking her red hair with one hand and drinking the milkshake with the other on the way to sewing lessons. No seat belts, no salmonella. I was the smallest child in my class, and these milkshakes were to be the solution.

"Teeny-tiny," screamed the boys. "You're as little as a bean." And I'd scream back, "Yeah, a human bean."

I leaned against the wall outside my classroom at the YMCA. My son was marching around in the wilds of Central Park with his beloved babysitter, and I had such a longing to hold him to keep him from falling, but also such a longing to be caressed by my students' stories once again.

I pushed open the door to return to class. In those early days of motherhood, and now as the cloak of widowhood was approaching, I felt that every night I fell apart a little bit. Hearing my students' tales stitched me back together.

Mother

What will we be doing when Willem dies? Where will we be? How will Jake react? These thoughts raced through my head, and I ran to the comfort of friends' stories.

"I was in a tree when I heard that my brother had died," said Connie to me over coffee. "I was up at boarding school and the headmistress came and told me."

Connie is now fifty-one. "I always feel like I let him down," she said, "because I wasn't there at the end. My mother told me he would live longer. They told me to go back to school, and I did what I was told."

David's mother died when he was ten years old. David is now a doctor at a New York hospital that specializes in cancer care. "What was the first thought you had when you heard the news?" I asked him.

"I'm embarrassed to say this," said David. "She had been sick with breast cancer for more than a year, but the very first thought I had was to wonder if I still had to empty the dishwasher every night."

"What do you mean?"

"Well, that was my job. And it seemed if your mother dies you were special, that different rules might apply."

I met Linda in Sallie's waiting room. "My mother died when I was six," she told me that afternoon. "After she died my father gave away all of her things. I have one barrette from my mother," said Linda, tapping her head. "I keep my hair long so I can wear it."

Family Room

have called and called upon my friend Mary my whole life. I had called her the day I first visited Willem's apartment on Saint Mark's Place in Greenwich Village. I'd said, "Guess what he has hanging on his wall?"

"A hockey stick," said Mary, miraculously.

"Yes," I said.

She said, "Marry him."

Mary and I had played field hockey in high school, but in Holland men play field hockey as well as women, and Willem was on a team that played in Brooklyn every Sunday morning—men from India, Pakistan, the Caribbean, and Tibet.

Now Mary is a doctor in a busy emergency room in Dallas. I was able to speak to her briefly on the phone, before she began a grueling all-nighter in the ER, where she would do everything from deliver babies to deal with gunshot wounds and teenagers who had sniffed glue from paper bags.

"What happens when you know somebody is dying?" I said.

"The family will have been put in what we call the Family Room, a special room near the ER. If I cannot leave the patient, I ask a nurse to prepare the family 'for the worst.' When the patient dies, I go immediately to the family. Because I work in the ER, it is very unusual for me to have ever met the patient or the family before."

"Who is usually there?" I asked.

"Families can range from one to about fifteen people. I introduce myself and say I have very bad news. Often the people who are already crying turn out to be neighbors or in-laws. When I have identified the spouse and children, I try to look at them all equally. I say that Mr. Smith has died or is dead, using some part of the verb 'to die' very early. After that I revert to terms like 'passed away' or 'gone.'"

"Do you see many young children in the Family Room?" I asked.

"Actually, I've never seen kids in the Family Room. I don't know why. I guess they're home with family or friends. I guess they don't want the children to hear the bad news," said Mary.

"Maybe it would be better if they were there, if the doctor could tell them and calmly explain what happened, rather than a crying parent," I said. "Let me know if there's ever a child there, and what you say to them."

"I'll tell you if it happens, but so far, in twenty years, it never has."

A Train

I was fifteen when Robert Kennedy was killed, and when I heard the news it was as if my lover had been shot. I had worshipped John Kennedy like a father, but I was "in love" with Bobby Kennedy. I had never taken the train to New York City alone, "the city," as we called it, but I convinced my parents that I had to go pay my respects to my sweetheart at Saint Patrick's Cathedral.

It was a warm June day, and I dressed carefully in a yellow and white flower print A-line dress I had struggled to make in home ec class. I wore a wide headband of matching fabric, with a messily sewn piece of elastic holding it together under my thick hair.

I took the 11:27 train to the city, and I sat on one of the wicker seats, diagonally across from a man who sat reading a thick hardback book. Just before we entered the tunnel into Manhattan, he quickly unzipped his pants and exposed himself. It was the first penis I'd ever seen. When we emerged from the tunnel at Grand Central Station, he sat perfectly dressed and zipped, reading his book.

I walked from Grand Central over to Fifth Avenue and up the eight blocks to Saint Patrick's Cathedral, as my mother had instructed. There I stood in line for three hours in the hot sun, waiting, waiting, waiting to see my beloved's coffin. I had told my parents I would take the 4:05 train home. There were people crying in line and other people playing the guitar and singing, and I spoke to nobody, because that's what I had promised my parents, but at one point a policeman walked up to me and asked where I was from, and we talked for fifteen minutes and I was smitten. At 3:30 I was two blocks away from Saint Patrick's and knew it would be two more hours before I got in, so I dutifully trudged back down Fifth Avenue to Grand Central, without seeing the man I loved. When I returned home I told my parents I had talked with a policeman and didn't get to see Robert Kennedy, but I did not tell them about the man on the train.

I gave the assignment of trains to my students.

Irene had been sitting at the kitchen table when the Nazis marched into Berlin. She was with her older brother and younger sister, and they were having dessert, her favorite, apple strudel with cinnamon and raisins. Her mother was at the sink. She remembers the Nazi knocking the strudel off the table with the butt of his rifle and screaming, "No time for dessert! No time for dessert! The train is leaving." That was the last time Irene saw her mother. As Irene read, her eyes teared. She whispered quietly that she never could eat desserts again.

I went around the table, calling on each student. Cynthia grew up in Rhode Island. She had just turned sixty and was perfectly coiffed, with a silk scarf around her neck and matching green leather purse and shoes.

"Cynthia, would you like to read?"

Cynthia hesitated. "My father," she began in a Jackie Kennedy whisper, "my father—this is very personal. It's not very good . . ."

"Would you like me to read it?" I said.

She nodded and passed her paper to me.

I cleared my throat and began to read aloud, not knowing what I would hear out of my own mouth. "My father took the train to work every morning. Our chauffeur drove him. Mummy was always having breakfast in bed when he left. Nony, our maid, served it to her on a mahogany tray. My sister and I would sit at the edge of her bed and read the funny papers before school. We thought this was a grand treat.

"One day the heavy black phone next to my

mother's bed rang. She waited two rings—she always did; she said she never wanted to sound too eager. She lifted the receiver to her ear. I'll never forget the look on her face.

"'Yes,' she murmured. 'Yes,' and shut her eyes. I don't know why, but I knew my father was dead when she said that. My father had told the chauffeur to hurry to catch the train, and they had driven fast over the tracks at the crossing. There was no crossing gate. The chauffeur said he had seen the train coming but my father had ordered him to drive fast across."

My voice wavered as I read Cynthia's story. "Thank you," I said when I finished it. "Thank you very much."

That day when I got home, Willem said to me, "I need to renew my driver's license, and next summer we'll go to Holland and then take a train to Brussels and rent a car. I want to show you Brussels, lieveling."

"Yes, lieveling," I promised, and we did renew his driver's license, although that next summer there would be no driving.

part three

Learning to Drive (or Not to Drive)

Eileen looked stunned in class when I gave the assignment of learning or not learning how to drive, but she bent her head to her paper immediately, and when she was done she asked if she could read first.

"My father would always scream at me when he was teaching me to drive," she read evenly. "He screamed if I drove too fast and he screamed if I drove too slow. I was always frightened with my father in the car, when he was at the wheel and when I was too. I failed the driving test twice because I was too scared to pass. Just now, as I write this, I remember a story I heard when I was a little girl. When my father learned to drive, the second time he was at the wheel, in a little town in Maine, he killed a child. I only heard the story once. My father died eight years ago. I wish I could have talked to him about it."

Then Leslie read. She was a modest sixty-year-old woman who wore matching sweaters and skirts to class. She laughed when she read, "My father didn't believe that women should learn to drive. So my mother would make me sleep in my clothes. Then she'd wake me at 3:00 a.m. and we'd sneak out and she let me drive the Dodge. She drove first, of course, away from the house, but when we got to the cemetery, that's where I drove. My father didn't know I'd gotten my driver's license until my wedding day."

My mother taught me how to drive when I was fourteen years old. We had a circular driveway, and I would drive my little sister around and around in the big blue Buick station wagon, peering through the steering wheel to see. Our favorite game was "mailman." I would stop the car at our mailbox and hand letters to my sister that I had carefully written to made-up people in foreign lands. After she placed them in the mailbox, she put up the little red metal flag to show the mailman there was mail to take. Of course, I was the mailman, so I had to drive around the driveway one more time to pick them up.

The Helpers of the Holy Souls owned two black cars. We called them the "nun cars." Whenever we saw one of the cars leave, the Mother Superior was always the one at the wheel, and she always wore sunglasses, rain or shine, when she drove. If I happened to be parked at the mailbox making a delivery or pickup, I solemnly waved to her as she passed and made my sister do the same. I prayed I would not go to hell for driving when I was only fourteen.

That same year that my mother taught me to drive, she gave me a book called *It's Time You Knew*, which was the same light blue as a Kotex box. The only line I remember is, "Remember, girls! Boys can be wolves, WOLVES IN THE BACK OF A CAR. NEVER, UNDER ANY CIRCUMSTANCE, GET IN THE BACK OF A CAR WITH A TEENAGE BOY!"

I longed to be in the back of a car with a teenage boy. Instead, I sat in the Buick with my sister at the mailbox and waved to Mother Superior and prayed she would not know what a sinner I was.

And now, when Willem and I walked out of the oncologist's office, where the doctor had gently suggested to Willem that he might not continue to drive, Willem said, "Lieveling, this is the hardest part of cancer for me."

A Strange Job

As Willem's health continued to decline, I began thinking about how I was going to support my son and myself. I would have a little life insurance from Willem, as well as a small pension from his employer. I reflected on the jobs I had had earlier in my life. One of the stranger jobs was reading questionnaires on male sexuality.

When I was twenty-four, I sat in a Central Park West office hour after hour with a large older woman, who probably was the age I am now, who wore her hair in long gray braids. We sat on filing cabinets and sifted through handwritten questionnaires about men's sexual habits for six hours a day. Some of the men's sexual activities were violent, and a surprising number were strange and involved bathtubs and animals, and it was our job to type these up. This was before computers. We didn't even have the beloved IBM Selectrics with their magical delete button, which would allow you to erase one letter at a time. This was the age of manual typewriters.

Our boss had been a model and was beautiful, with red hair and red lipstick. She would come in at the end of each day and throw her Bergdorf Goodman and Henri Bendel shopping bags on the floor and shout, "How's it going, girls?"

My first job was in high school working in a store that sold ski equipment and ski clothes. The boys sold equipment upstairs and the girls sold clothes downstairs. I was told to say, "It is expensive, but it's warm, and when you're on the slopes, you'll be thankful you have it."

I was also told to ask the men if they needed help zipping their ski parkas.

My second job was the summer of my senior year, working at a stationery store on an old-fashioned cash register. To get the job, I had to look up five names in the phone book as fast as I could. The man who hired me said, "You know the alphabet goddamn fast, goddamn fast. Can you sew? My wife doesn't do a damn thing. I have to hem my pants with staples."

I looked down, and indeed his wrinkled trousers were stapled around the cuffs. All that summer I handed *Playboy* magazines in paper bags to nervous men and listened to my boss talk about his "goddamned wife."

These were not the jobs I aspired to. I wanted to be Harriet Tubman. I wanted to be Joan of Arc. Now my husband was leaving me and I just needed to make a plan.

A Letter

Willem and I loved each other, but we never had an easy time talking. It was partially the fact that I spoke no Dutch and he had learned English as an adult. I often felt that our conversations were like a broken zipper that always got stuck unexpectedly when we talked. A friend, Eva, who had also married a Dutchman, once said, "It's deceptive that these guys speak English; basically their culture is as foreign as if we had married someone from Japan."

In the first year of our marriage Willem returned to Amsterdam to do research for three months, and we each sent postcards we got from museums every single day. Those postcards are my most cherished possessions. And when he returned we continued the practice, not every day, but we often wrote each other postcards, stamped them, and dropped them in the mailbox as if we didn't live in the same home.

We even went so far, when we were at home together and unable to communicate well, as to sit at the kitchen table with a piece of paper between us. We would take turns writing what was bothering us, and then slide the paper to the other to get a response.

Five months after Willem asked what a car seat was, I woke up at 3:00 a.m. with a start, gasping for air. He happened to be sleeping soundly that night, and as I watched him, I vowed that when he woke I would ask him to write Jake a letter to give him on his thirteenth birthday. If he could hand deliver it, that would be lovely, and if not, Jake would still have his words. But then I immediately realized he would get upset by my request, so I decided to ask everybody in my family to write a letter. Who knows what will happen to any of us at any time? I reasoned. It's just a good thing to do.

I now have in a folder in my filing cabinet five letters written to Jake. Some of those people have died; some are still alive.

A Closet

The autumn I turned sixteen I was so irritable that my parents sent me to London to live with old friends of theirs, who were physicians, and their three children. During World War II, my mother had been a pen pal with the wife's brother, and their crinkly aerogrammes lay in a cigar box in our attic when I was growing up. I had dreams of a hippie school, but my parents sent me to North London Collegiate School for Girls, where I wore a brown uniform and trudged though the rain to the tube every day. At North London Collegiate we were not allowed to wear our "outside" shoes when we were inside; instead we had to wear plimsolls, what Americans called sneakers.

The first dreary morning, I was at the school surrounded by an army of girls in their brown uniforms when the form mistress (class teacher) said firmly, "Jewish girls raise your hands." I hesitated. I didn't know what they would do with me if I raised my hand.

Four girls raised their hands.

"Stand, please," the form mistress commanded.

This was 1969. "Go to Jewish prayers," she ordered, as if they were being sent to the tower, and they filed out, two with dark curls, one ethereal blonde, and one bold orange-haired girl.

"Now we can begin *our* prayers," she said, and launched into the Lord's Prayer.

Each morning for three weeks I sat through Christian prayers, until one morning the form mistress cornered me and said, "Jewesses must go to Jewish prayers."

I was raging with adolescent torment, and the whole year I was so off balance I never got my period. I had packed half my suitcase with two large light blue boxes of Kotex. Each month I waited and waited and was relieved and frightened, although I had only gone as far as second base and was fairly certain I could not be pregnant. The day before the flight back to New York after my year abroad, I stealthily stuffed a handful of the Kotex pads into my pocketbook, and when I was certain nobody was looking, I threw them into separate wastebaskets on the rolling lawns of Hampstead Heath. It took eight trips to dispose of them all. Then I crushed the light blue boxes and put them at the bottom of my suitcase and brought them back to America.

I did almost lose my virginity in London. One

night the father of the family I was staying with took me to some kind of medical meeting, although I'm not sure why. One of his young colleagues, a doctor in his twenties, asked me which Beatle I preferred. I said "Paul," and then he invited me for a ginger beer with him after the meeting. He said he would give me a lift home.

The young doctor, who was fifteen years my senior, took me back to his ice-cold flat and asked if I wanted to go to bed with him. I said I was cold, and he said I could have one of his wife's sweaters. I was stunned when he opened a closet full of women's clothes. "My wife died a few months ago of leukemia," he said quietly.

I put on one of her sweaters, a gray wool cardigan, and we got into bed with all of our clothes on and hugged. The doctor cried, I stroked his hair, and then he drove me back to where I was staying. It was not the thought of sleeping with a stranger, an older man, that shocked me as much as the dead wife's clothes in the closet. I had no idea that thirty years later I would have my dead husband's clothes in my closet or that, by that time, it would not shock me at all.

Fire Truck

A week before Jake's fourth birthday, he announced he wanted a cake in the shape of a fire truck. I am not a baker. I have the urge to bake perhaps twice a year, and that usually results in an apple or a pumpkin pie with, I confess, store-bought crust. But my son wanted a cake in the shape of a fire truck, and in that way that mothers are able to lift cars off their children's feet in an emergency, I somehow made one. I used practically a whole bottle of red dye in the frosting, which in earlier days would appall me, but now I reasoned that if Willem grew up on the purest whole wheat bread and beet salad, perhaps junk food was the key to a long life. I decorated the cake with care—licorice hoses, peppermint wheels, butterscotch headlights, and a lattice of thin pretzels for ladders. It was my offering to my son on what I knew would be his last birthday with his father.

We had the party in Central Park. On a glistening October day, friends helped push carts containing the food and party favors to Central Park. Willem was able to walk there slowly, but with elegance, holding my hand, wearing his navy blue Nike headband on his head, which he'd worn since his first surgery to cover his scar.

After the children played an endless game of freeze tag, they gathered around a picnic table we'd covered with a pumpkin-colored paper tablecloth. I carefully placed the fire truck cake in front of Jake, then lit the candles as the children jumped up and down. Jake shut his eyes and made a wish, then opened them and blew out all the candles. Ever since, he makes wishes whenever candles are lit and on eyelashes and fluffy dandelions. "I always make the same wish, Mom," he says, "and you can't ever ask me what it is."

Laundry

efore we could get out the door—me to take Willem to his third surgery and the babysitter to take Jake to preschool—Jake cried, "I want to take the training wheels off my bike! Right now!" As we stood there, the three of us knew (Willem as his mind drifted away, I with my somewhat addled mind, and Jake in his four-year-old wisdom) that Willem would not be the one who took them off. With that thought I took Willem to the hospital.

In the middle of the endless operation I felt a chill in my soul that it was not going well. I sat rocking back and forth in the cold waiting room and then suddenly fled home. The only thing I could think to do was put a load of laundry in the washing machine before I returned to the hospital. Doing that task grounded me.

Willem emerged alive from the surgery but spoke gibberish for three days. The left side of his body was paralyzed. That night at home, as I sat with Jake on my lap in his bedroom, I said quietly, "Daddy might die in the hospital."

When I asked him if he wanted to visit Willem, he climbed down and went into his closet and shut the door.

"I want privacy," he announced.

Minutes later he emerged with a button-down shirt on, buttoned perfectly, a shirt I'd bought a year before when this mess started. I kept thinking that if I was prepared with the little things, clothes for the funeral, a cemetery plot, like checking off the list of supplies for school, then I might stave off death. I had never mentioned this shirt to Jake, and he always insisted on T-shirts, but there he was in that shirt ready to visit his father, and he insisted on sleeping in it as well.

The next morning I took Jake to the hospital, and he sat on Willem's bed while they both struggled with the small containers of red Jell-O and talked a garbled Dutch to each other.

When Willem came home from this surgery, he needed to be in a hospital bed. My husband and I no longer shared a bed.

A Fish

Sallie posed a question to a women's group she was part of. "What was your first memory of loss?"

A fit woman in her forties shook her head and apologized, "I don't think I helped my four-year-old's first loss. His goldfish died last month. I flushed it down the toilet but didn't have the heart to tell him that he had died or what I had done with him, so I said, 'The goldfish went on vacation.'"

Another woman in her sixties said, "Well, I can't think of one, but my husband's mother died when he was six, and kids weren't allowed in the hospital at the time, so he stood across the street and waved up at her. That's how he said good-bye to his mother. He says he thinks about that all the time."

Snow

I n January of 1998 Willem won a raffle at his office for two round-trip tickets to Paris. Paris with a three-year-old did not seem particularly romantic, but it took us until November to get the nerve to leave Jake for four days with his beloved babysitter, Rosane.

As we walked around the streets of Paris, Willem would say almost inaudibly, "Snow. It's going to snow. I'm cold." It was freezing cold, it did snow, the Louvre was on strike, and we had picnic dinners in our room each night because the hotel and airfare were paid for but not food. They were four of the happiest days of my life.

We did not yet know Willem had cancer. Looking back, his whispering about the cold may have been the first sign that he might be ill. He never had complained about the cold before.

In the winters of my childhood, at night I'd hear the deer clamber up our porch steps when it snowed. While it was still dark in the morning, we could hear the scraping of snowplows through the snowy streets. On those days I leaped out of bed quicker than usual to listen to the radio. The list of school closings in towns sounded like a jump rope chant, and if they called out our town, I'd cheer, "A snow day!" and throw my pillow in the air.

After oatmeal I would stuff myself into snow clothes and boots and trudge through the snowdrifts to the Helpers of the Holy Souls. The convent was never officially closed, but it was never open either. As I stood looking over their grounds, I could tell that something secret was going on. The nuns were preparing to go sledding. They usually had three wooden toboggans leaning against the side of the chapel. In spring they stood out like gargoyles guarding the place. In summer, vines would grow through them. In fall they were strewn with autumn leaves. But on those special winter days they would be gone. I never saw the nuns take them, but I could hear their laughter as they hurled themselves down the snowy hill, and I would run over there, hide behind the big copper beech tree, and watch them, their habits sailing black against the white, white snow.

In Holland Willem had a bicycle the size of a horse, and he tethered huge lamb's wool gloves to the handlebars so that he could slide his hands into them on the frosty days he cycled along the canals to school.

He said some days the gloves were crusted with ice crystals like jewels. He also had a map stand on the handlebars, where he would prop a guide to the intricate weavings of the bike trails. He knew all the back ways, but he said having a map made him feel like an explorer rather than a skinny student cycling to school along the icy canals.

Hardware Store

n those months at the end of Willem's life, one of the things that sustained Jake was the hardware store. Every day after I picked him up from pre-school we walked past the Aquarius Hardware Store on Ninetieth Street and Columbus Avenue. Perhaps it had some cosmic powers, but whatever the reason, Jake would pull my arm in a tug-of-war. I relented, usually, partially because I didn't want to hurt my arm but also because I have happy memories of walking the aisles of my hometown hardware store with my father when I was a child, breathing in the smell of 3-in-One oil, running my hands over the open bins of nails.

Jake often wanted an amulet from the store, inexpensive things, and again, I usually gave in. We still have four tape measures, three egg timers, and one hundred yards of yellow DANGER WET PAINT tape from those days.

For me it was the smell of basil that would help me carry on. Every week that Willem was sick, for fifteen months, I bought a bunch of fresh basil at the grocery store, and it was more precious to me than a bouquet of roses.

At night, when Willem and Jake were finally asleep, I would sneak into the kitchen and hold the basil to my nose. I would shut my eyes, inhale it, and imagine someday picking fresh basil and tomatoes from a summer garden.

Sticks and Stones

One spring morning Jake woke up and climbed into my bed. "I think Daddy is doing 'the leaving part' now," he whispered. From then on, everything Willem touched, and everything Willem wore, became a totem. Jake began asking to put on our wedding rings for a few minutes before he fell asleep.

Each time he visited Sallie now he would say goodbye to her, ride his bike halfway down the block, and say, "I forgot the sticks and leaves." Then we'd pivot, as if in a choreographed dance, and walk back to her office, scanning the sidewalk for stray sticks and leaves. He would study them carefully and select the correct ones; then I'd hold his bicycle while he went back to give them to Sallie.

Willem went through a stage of sorting through everything he owned and throwing away any shred of paper he deemed not necessary. When one of Willem's sisters, Marjon, visited from Holland, she and Jake decided to do the opposite in Jake's room, which had always been sparely decorated with two Babar posters. Jake sat on her tall shoulders and taped his artwork on the walls like a collage, all the way up to the ceiling. Jake had now officially declared his room his own territory.

A week before Willem died, Jake went into my bedroom and shut the door.

"Don't come in," he insisted, and I gave him a few minutes alone. Willem was asleep in the hospital bed in the extra room.

"Okay," Jake shouted, "it's ready."

When I walked in he held out his hand and pointed to the bed, as if he were presenting a masterpiece.

On the bed were stones and beach glass from a bowl I kept by the window. The stones and glass were lined up in an orderly and intricate pattern. For the next few days I had to carefully move them to Willem's now empty side of the bed before I slept, and each morning Jake methodically put them back.

A Honeymoon

When Willem and I were on our honeymoon on St. Eustatius, we stayed at an inn run by an English couple. The third bristling-hot afternoon, while Willem lay naked on the canopy bed with the ceiling fan whirring, reading about the seventeenth-century Dutch in Brooklyn, I drifted down to the small terra-cotta lobby to get some ice. As I was wrestling with the ice machine, which was spewing ice out onto the floor, the sixty-year-old redheaded Englishwoman at the desk said, "I'm so glad you're here on a honeymoon. Honeymoons make me happy." Then, turning to the ice machine, she said, "That always happens," and she came to my aid, throwing the ice out into the bougainvillea bushes.

I smiled and bent to help scoop up the ice, but she obviously wanted to talk more.

"I once was very much in love with a beautiful young man," she said, as though we were in a play, "and he was killed in a car crash. I vowed I would get my driver's license and learn to drive so I could take my own life in the same way. Do you know what happened?"

She stood up, wiped her hands on her cotton dress, and rang the bell on the desk for emphasis. "I fell in love with the driving instructor. I did! That's my Thomas," she beamed, pointing to the photo of her and her husband on the wall. "We moved here from England ten years ago."

A Painting

As Willem's memory slipped away in the night-time sky, every day there was less he would recall of his everyday life, his past, our son's babyhood. One day Jake and I sat at the window, gazing out at the buildings, at seagulls, and at the little swatch of the Hudson River that we could see. We sat to paint, using the radiator cover as our easel.

"I see a sailboat!" screamed Jake. "I'll paint it, and then when it sails away it will be saved!" he said as he painted a radiant orange sail.

The next day Jake stepped on Willem's foot while Willem was sitting in his wheelchair. Willem screamed a swearword in Dutch. Jake screamed back another swearword in Dutch. When I asked Jake to make up with his father, he said, "I might have used up all of my kisses." For fourteen months the doctor had asked me, "Can Willem still play with his son?" and I'd been surprised by the question, but now I understood. "No," I would have said, if there had been a doctor in the house to talk to.

But then I told them both a story about when Jake was a baby and Willem took him out in his backpack and they both came back with snow in their eyelashes. Telling them both a story about their lives, a story neither of them remembered, calmed them down, and Jake climbed onto Willem's lap and they hugged.

Perfume

The first summer Willem and I were married we stayed in a cottage in the village of Marum, in Friesland, which is in the north of Holland. Friesland is home to some of the tallest people in the world. They often stared at me, though not unkindly, a five-foot bride, struggling to keep up on a too-large bicycle. We didn't have a car and cycled everywhere.

Every night we had dinner of fresh fish from the lakes and ripe strawberries and ate outside at the Ping-Pong table in the garden, lingering in the evening sunlight until 10:00 p.m. The village had three stores, and at the grocery store there was a large glass container full of violet perfume, where the ladies of the town filled and refilled their variously shaped bottles.

As Willem studied his maps, I filled an old Noxzema jar full of violet perfume so I could anoint my body. Our two weeks in Friesland felt enchanted.

My grandmother used to say, "The tide goes in, and the tide goes out. You have to bend your knee and ride the waves." Now, with Willem down the hall in his hospital bed, I could feel the tide taking us out. Thinking about the outcome, after several sleepless hours of lying diagonally in our bed alone, I got up and ransacked the drawers until I found that now-empty Noxzema jar and tried to inhale the violet smell.

A Cartwheel

At breakfast Willem said something to me, and I had to ask him to repeat himself three times, and each time I tried to do it without raising my voice or changing my tone. And finally I understood what he was saying.

"I've finished my work here," he said, pointing to his books and papers. "I'm done."

As I walked Jake to day camp that morning, he said, "There's no gas or air or air-conditioning on Jupiter."

I waited all day at Willem's bedside, except for when I picked up Jake from camp.

When Jake went in to kiss his father good night, Willem said, "I don't know if I'll be here in the morning."

When I put Jake to bed, he said, "Where would he be?" and I explained that Willem was going to die very soon.

Jake said, "I think he's very tired."

After Jake finally went to sleep in his room, I went back to Willem. "I'm sorry," he said. "Is it okay if I die?"

"Yes," I whispered. "I'll take care of Jake."

That morning Willem woke up at 4:00 yelling. He was definitely still there.

While Jake was at camp I bought him a red scooter because I needed to celebrate something. That evening we took turns riding it on the wide sidewalk in front of our building. It was like sailing, gliding along as my husband lay dying upstairs.

When we got back inside, Jake went to Willem's bed and said, "Daddy, I have a loose tooth, a loose tooth. Do tooth fairies come to alligators, too?"

It was the first time I saw Willem smile in several weeks, a half smile, on one side of his face. Also that night Willem stopped eating, and Jake did the best cartwheel he'd ever done.

A Bed

Nurses came in to help. I could not lift my husband, and that was what I needed now. Not moral support, not words of comfort, people who were physically strong.

The day nurse, Constance, from Trinidad, laughed and said, "I can't imagine some white woman coming to live with us, to help out. We're born at home and we die at home. It's nothing to be ashamed of. There were eleven of us kids. Some lived long. Some died young. That's nature."

Willem was born in his parents' bed in a village called Utingeradeel, in Friesland. He was the oldest, and when his first two sisters were born, he was sent to stay with relatives during their births. When his mother went into labor with his third sister, he was told to go to the baker and get a basket of bread. When he returned, there was the new baby on his parents' bed. He says he remembers standing there with the basket full of fresh bread, meeting his beautiful new sister.

There was no question for Willem or me that he would die at home. The doctor warned us, "I don't know if this is something a child should see."

Of course, it was August and we would much prefer to have been at the beach, much prefer for Willem to jump in the waves with Jake, much prefer any of it compared with watching him die, but "that's the deal," as Jake had just learned to say. Strangely, as upsetting as it was, it seemed the natural thing to happen at this point. After all this unraveling, after Willem slowly and not so slowly lost his languages and mind, it seemed the natural thing for him to leave life.

I told the hospice worker, an energetic woman who arrived twice a week and spent her life helping people die, that Willem would die very soon.

"Oh, no," she insisted. "He could be with us for a few more months."

"No," I said firmly. "I can feel him leaving."

I'd never watched someone die, but I could feel it inside me, as powerfully as sex. I could feel my life telescoping—becoming a widow slowly at first, and now more quickly. Willem's language had crumbled. He knew Dutch, English, French, Italian, German, Latin, and ancient Greek, and it was all moving from him so swiftly, as if workmen were hurling shelf after shelf of books from the windows of a beautiful house. Meanwhile Jake was exploding with language. "Stegosaurus," "combine harvester," "islands of the Bahamas."

An Elevator

At five o'clock on a hot afternoon, I picked up Jake from camp and we stopped at the hardware store. He selected two choice pieces of sandpaper, and we returned home.

Willem lay on the hospital bed in the guest room, where he'd been the past three weeks. Jake waved to him and went in to tell him about kickball and swimming; Willem didn't speak but moved his hand slightly. Then Jake and I went into the living room and sat on the couch watching a Blue's Clues video from the library. The tape was wobbly. After a few minutes I had to get up to adjust the tracking, then I went in to check on Willem.

He lay there still as a board. His breathing was shallow, like fluttering moths. He had turned his hands inward. I touched his feet and they were ice cold.

I went back to Jake. I felt extremely calm, as if this were the natural place where we had been heading. "Daddy's going to stop breathing soon," I said.

"How do you know?" he asked. Then he whispered, "Don't turn off the video."

"Come with me," I said, putting out my hand.

Jake climbed on Willem's bed and kissed his face all over. Then Willem stopped breathing. Jake and I looked at each other.

"I guess you won't have anymore birthday parties, Daddy," Jake said solemnly. Then he jumped off the bed and showed off his cartwheels.

I called the funeral home, a number I had written down fifteen months before, and had kept tucked in my address book.

"We can come right over ma'am," they said eagerly.

"No, please," I said. "Please give us two hours."

I have no idea where I got that amount of time.

Now a thunderstorm was crashing outside, cooling down the summer evening. I had the urge to run out and get the clothes off the line, although we lived on the sixteenth floor and had no clothesline.

I cannot account exactly for those two hours. Jake and I stayed in the room with Willem. It was strangely peaceful, as the thunder crashed and the rain came down, and Jake did cartwheel after cartwheel.

Two hours exactly after I called the funeral parlor, two men in suits, who appeared to be from the 1950s, were at the door, shaking rain off themselves.

Jake kept saying, "How are you going to fit Daddy out the door?" but the men did not respond.

Eventually they tipped him up out the door and took him in the elevator. They managed. There wasn't room for us in that elevator, so we waited for it to come back up.

When we took the elevator down, Jake and I held hands, and Jake began to sing "Frère Jacques," which was the first song Willem and I ever sang to him. I sang along with him until we reached the ground floor. When we got outside, the two men in suits were placing Willem in the back of a black van. I remember being surprised that it was a van, not a hearse.

That night I lay with Jake in his bed and we held each other as the rain pounded down.

"Now we're two," said Jake.

"What?" I said.

"Now we're two people," he said softly.

part four

A Shovel

On the day of Willem's funeral, I couldn't get Jake to wear what he called his "lots of buttons shirt," but he did acquiesce to a navy blue polo shirt with three buttons. Willem's three tall sisters were there from Holland, and the youngest of the three carried Jake the four blocks to the funeral home.

During the funeral, when Willem's friends were eulogizing him, Jake began to lose patience and tugged on my arm.

"I want to go to the digging part," he said.

Finally we drove out of the city, dazed and weary, to the cemetery on a hill where Willem and I had blithely picked out a spot and had a romantic afternoon only months before. A sweet wind blew in the August afternoon.

We all took turns shoveling, in the way the rabbi had instructed, with the backside of the shovel to show this was a special kind of digging. And then, and then, a picture I thought I'd never see, my four-year-old son reached for the shovel and he, too, dumped two shovelfuls of dirt onto his father's plain pine coffin.

A train whistled in the valley below us, and Jake handed the shovel to his cousin and put his arms straight up in the air. I knew what he wanted. I lifted him up as the rabbi said prayers, and we watched the train snaking by. I held him tight and we waved to the far-off travelers.

A Lost Tooth

Five days after Willem died, at six o'clock in the evening, when the sun still shone brightly, I was playing Candyland with Jake in his bedroom when one of his baby teeth fell out onto the board, right on my favorite picture of a chocolate bar. Jake was ecstatic, and he proudly picked up the tooth and immediately ran to hide it under his pillow, on top of the photo of his father and him bottle-feeding a baby lamb.

That night, when Jake was asleep and the apartment was far too quiet, I stood alone in the living room, staring out at the Hudson River; I could see the lights of one lone tugboat slowly making its way to the Atlantic Ocean.

"I am a single mother now," I whispered as I got one dollar from my wallet. I had the urge to give Jake something from Willem, something Willem had touched. I rooted around in my underwear drawer and found a small shell he'd found for me on Shelter Island years ago, when our biggest challenge was getting sand off our feet before we leaped into bed. I slid my hand under my son's pillow, grabbed the tiny tooth, and quietly left the dollar and the shell.

My son was sleeping with his beloved stuffed dog in one hand, and I realized he was also clutching a tape recording of my husband reading *Curious George* to him in Dutch.

A Newspaper

My mother worked for the local small-town newspaper, the *Patent Trader*, writing a column (before psychedelic drugs were popular, or before we knew they were popular) called "Tripping Lightly" about where to go on one-day adventures within a forty-mile radius of our small town. Some mornings my mother would wake me from my childhood slumber to explore the old Fulton Fish Market before dawn, the colonial restorations where women in eighteenth-century garb chatted earnestly as they churned butter, or the riverbed where a trove of Indian arrowheads had just been unearthed. I would bring along my notebook and pen and religiously take notes along with my mother.

My grandfather had a newspaper column in the *Printing News* called "Salesman Sam." Each month he doled out advice on how to live one's life, taken from his own personal experiences, ranging from having to go to work when he was twelve years old after his father died to building and running his own successful paper company. He would also include advice from his personal heroes, Benjamin Franklin and Thomas Alva Edison, or Alva, as my grandfather referred to him.

When I was growing up next door to the convent, a newspaper boy would deliver the *New York Times* and the *Patent Trader*. I was in love with the newspaper boy, and I wanted to be a newspaper boy myself. For my tenth birthday I got bike baskets that fit on the sides over my back tire. For the following weeks, until the neighbors complained, I rode gallantly around the neighborhood hurling old newspapers onto people's front lawns.

My husband had a passion for newspapers, and he would clip articles, meticulously and endlessly, on Dutch history, the Dutch soccer team Ajax, and everything in the world that contained the word *Judaica*. He brought a pair of scissors along on our honeymoon, and that first married summer in the north of Holland, he rode his bicycle thirty kilometers to the nearest big town, Leuwarden, early one morning to get newspapers as I slept.

I clipped my husband's obituary carefully with my husband's special clipping scissors. Sitting at the kitchen table, it was surreal reading his obituary in the newspaper. I remember reading it and rereading it. Friends had paid for it to be in the *New York Times*. It was technically an announcement, not an obituary.

He was not a famous man, so it was short, about his being a historian and an archivist, husband and father and brother. Along with this necessary information, our friends had also included, "and he always called pinecones 'pineapples,'" which brought me back to leaving the orphanage with our son. Something had caught in the wheel spokes of the stroller, and my husband had said, "a pineapple," and that small pinecone sits on my desk today.

I clipped my husband's obituary carefully with my husband's special clipping scissors. At first I wasn't sure where to put it, but then I filed it in the folder he had carefully labeled FRIENDS.

A Traffic Jam

A month after Willem died, Jake woke up and announced, "I want to go to Antarctica with Winnie the Pooh and Eeyore, even though he complains."

The house felt calm. A friend told me it is Jewish custom to walk around the block or neighborhood to represent reentry into society, which I did, alone, walking quietly on the sidewalk where Jake had taken his first steps.

The next day Jake had an appointment with Sallie. I sat in the waiting room and fell asleep, the first peaceful rest I'd had in months. When Jake burst out of the room, carrying one of his precious little Jeeps, he went to feed the fish in the fish tank as he always did.

Sallie motioned to me, and I looked into her room where they'd been. There was an ornate but perfectly arranged traffic jam stretching the length of the room, all the cars facing front.

"For months," she said quietly, "he has been making car crashes, and now it's all in order."

"I feel that way, too," I said.

A Playground

I f I were in a small town or out in the country, I might not meet other women daily among the jungle gyms. If I lived in a house, I would be staring out my solitary kitchen window as Jake and a friend horsed around in the backyard. In New York the playground is our common backyard, and we join our children there. I'm not wearing a *W* emblazoned on my chest, but I'm there as the kids swing, chit-chatting with the married mothers who complain about their husbands.

I admit that when Willem was alive, I felt free to talk about the frustrations of marriage. Widowhood is a curious cloak to wear when you are a mother with a young kid. People are extraordinarily kind and generous to widows, picking up our children from school, slicing the birthday cake, and taking off training wheels. Now that I'm a widow, I don't know what to say to those with living husbands any more than they know what to say to me. Simple conversations can be startling if someone doesn't know you're a widow.

Two weeks after Willem died, I was standing on the playground when a woman shielded her toddler from a hurled ball and said, "Don't you hate it when your husband is home for lunch?"

I, without the usual, "Well, I have a different situation . . ." just blurted out, "Actually my husband's dead, and I'd give anything to have a sandwich with him just once again."

A Shopping Bag

Sallie was working with a number of children who'd lost parents to cancer and broached the possibility of us parents meeting one another. She got no opposition.

Five months after Willem died, on a cold night in December, while Jake was playing Candyland with a babysitter, I thrashed around in my room trying on clothes and then hurling them to the floor. What does a widow wear? I'd read that in a village in England in the nineteenth century widows wore black for the first year and lavender the year after that. I had done research on widows. In India, Hindu women really are supposed to "manifest inconsolable grief for the rest of their lives" after their husbands die. In Swaziland, widows wear a heavy saddle of twisted grass.

I did not wear a saddle of twisted grass to that meeting but settled on a pair of black pants and a heron blue sweater that I'd always liked, which was Willem's favorite color. I wore my hair back in a ponytail and vowed that soon, soon, I would get a grown-up haircut.

I hurried up Broadway to Ninety-fifth Street in the icy air. The meeting was held in an upstairs office in the brownstone where Sallie had her office. As I walked up the stairs I heard Sallie talking to a man, and I said the word "widower" out loud to myself. I opened the door and saw that Sallie was making tea for him, a jovial, dark-haired man, who put out his hand to greet me. His name was Steve. A moment later two more people entered the room, first a beautiful svelte woman of about forty, dressed in a stunning red coat and high black boots. When she opened her coat she revealed a chic, tailored suit. No widow's weeds for her.

She put out her hand. "Hi, I'm Lydia," she said, and it soon turned out our boys were in the same class at school.

Then there was Chris, who, although ten years younger, bore a startling resemblance to Willem. He was more than six feet tall and fine featured, and he was carrying a large shopping bag from Toys "R" Us. I blushed when I saw him.

We all made nervous chitchat while Sallie was a gracious hostess, offering hot cups of tea all around. When we finally settled down, we introduced ourselves more formally, or, rather, we gave the reasons why we were all in that little room.

Steve's wife, a healthy, vibrant nonsmoker, had complained of a backache. She went to a chiropractor, then her internist, and within three months she had died of lung cancer. They had an eleven-year-old son.

Lydia and her husband had three children. They had lived in Hawaii, had traveled all over the world, and were still madly in love when he died of pancreatic cancer.

Chris's wife, his college sweetheart, died next to him in bed after a year under siege with colon cancer. They had two teenage daughters.

Each of us alternately wept openly and held back tears, but no matter what the outward appearance, the walls that night contained the sorrows we all felt. It was as if by telling our stories, and knowing that Sallie knew all of our children so well, we had entered some safe and rare sanctuary.

"So what's in the bag?" Sallie asked jokingly as we were getting ready to leave. "Christmas presents for us?"

Chris turned red. "No, well, actually, no. It's my wife's ashes. Well, half of them. She was Belgian and we're bringing them to her parents in Brussels over the holidays."

We all looked at one another in horror for one moment, and then, in an instant, we all, including

Chris, exploded into laughter. The balance between heartbreaking and hysterical has united this little group forever.

Heaven

I personally have always liked the notion of Heaven, although I don't follow any rules of religion. After Willem died, I used to read Jake a children's story about how some people believe your soul floats up into the sky after you die, and it made Heaven sound very appealing, with puffy clouds and smiling cherubs. Jake asked me to read this book many times, and I obliged.

One night Jake requested the book again. I sat on his bed, reading the book so slowly and carefully I almost nodded off myself. After I finished reading the book and closed it, Jake was silent. I assumed he was asleep, but as I kissed his little forehead he said, "Well, we had a Kevin in our class," and I realized this whole time he had been confusing the words "Heaven" and "Kevin."

For six months after Willem died, at bedtime I stood with Jake at his bedroom window and we talked about our day, which I thought was a nice ritual, and I even had the wild thought that Willem might hear us as we looked at the nighttime sky.

Then one night, after I recounted a particularly

poignant moment on the playground, when Jake had swung from the rings to the jungle gym, Jake said to me, "Mom, I don't know who you're talking to. Daddy's in a box in the ground."

So Heaven hasn't gotten much mileage in our house, but I know for many people it does. My friend Beth's first-grade daughter went to school one day to learn that her thirty-two-year-old teacher had died suddenly, not in class, but of a heart attack at home.

The whole school mourned, and a week after the funeral, Beth's daughter came home from school after a day with the substitute teacher and said sadly, "I miss Miss Thomas."

"So do I," said Beth. "But what made you miss her today?"

Her daughter stretched out her little leg. "She didn't get to see my new shoes," she said wistfully, and then she looked heavenward and pointed down to her feet, hoping her teacher might catch a glimpse.

A Ride

T here were many nights when Jake would suddenly burst into tears, weeping for his father, which of course broke my heart. My head was filled with large and unanswerable questions. How can my dear child bear this pain? How can I comfort him? Who will comfort him when I die? On and on and on. But when I took Sallie's advice and said simply, "What would you do if Daddy were here?" he stopped crying and said calmly, "I'd ask him for a ride on his shoulders."

Simple things. Concrete things.

The actor who played the beloved character of Mr. Hooper on *Sesame Street* died in 1976. How were they going to convey this to the viewers, most of them under six years old? There were meetings, memos, and anguished arguments. Should they rewrite the story, showing that Mr. Hooper went away on a trip? Should they get a new actor and never tell the children, hoping they wouldn't know the difference?

In the end, after hours of discussion, they settled on three things: (1) write into the script that the actor playing Mr. Hooper had died, (2) show the other members of the cast being sad, and (3) have them say they would miss him.

No lies, nothing elaborate.

I know a filmmaker who has traveled all over the world, in war zones and areas of horrible deprivation, and he says he is constantly struck by how surprised Americans are by death compared with people from other countries. One afternoon he said to me, "In other countries everybody seems to know early on that everybody dies. I'm still trying to figure out why Americans have trouble with this concept, but I haven't a clue."

A Kitchen

Sallie and I have both begun asking people about their first memories of death, and we're startled to hear not only how so often the death was not discussed or the funeral was considered not a fit place for children but also how in some cases it was as if the adults pretended the death hadn't happened. The show had to go on.

When Kathleen's mother died in a small town in Ireland, Kathleen was not allowed to attend the funeral. She and her sisters were instructed to "be good" and stay inside at their aunt's house. When the funeral procession passed right by their front yard, the girls were told not to look out the window, and they obeyed.

Ken's grandmother lived with them while he was growing up. She had Alzheimer's disease and had a bed in the kitchen so everybody could keep an eye on her. She died on that bed in that kitchen. Ken was twelve years old at the time, and his father was director of a youth group that was scheduled to go to Disney World on the day she died.

"It's hard to believe," said Ken, shaking his head,

"but my father put my mother in charge of everything—the body, the funeral home, the funeral—and he and I went with the group to Disney World!"

John grew up in South Carolina. He shared a room with his little brother, but when his brother died of brain cancer, everything, including all of his toys, was taken away. "No trace," says John, as if in a trance. "My father sat out in the backyard for a week and didn't speak to us. It was just before Christmas. Then we celebrated Christmas as if nothing had happened. My brother's name was never said out loud again."

Cigarette, Cigar, Pipe

When I smell cigar smoke, I see my grandfather, Sam Himmell, who started his own paper company.

"Paper is good because it's clean," he said. "It's a good, clean business."

He lived to be ninety-three years old. When Willem died, Jake said, "How come grandpa got to be ninety-four and Daddy was only fifty?"

"I don't know," I murmured. "I just don't know."

"I know, I know," said my son. "I think sometimes God runs out of numbers."

On rainy summer days my grandfather would dance on the screen porch wearing his bathing suit and top hat, with the Victrola playing a scratchy Benny Goodman record. He would hold a shiny cane in one hand and a cigar in the other. The smell of the cigar and the rain, moths clinging to the screen in the evenings, my aunts and uncles playing cards on the porch, the cousins playing freeze tag nearby, these brief moments of family; the smell of a cigar brings these occasions back when I walk down the sidewalk.

My son has a smaller family, but he still has one grandfather. When we visit him, he lets Jake sit on his lap and drive the car along the back roads, and when they return to the house they don't get out of the car right away. They sit in the driveway with the doors open like wings. I look out the kitchen window and have no idea what they're talking about. But I am happy they talk, and later Jake says, "Grandpa takes me to a secret pond and he talks to me about olden-day stuff," and I hope Jake will remember that stuff forever.

The Moon

Seven weeks after Willem died, I gave my students the assignment "Memory of the Moon," because on nights Jake especially missed his father, he talked about "the man in the moon." I couldn't resist sneaking a look through the window in the classroom door as my students bent their heads to their papers. I love to watch people write, physically write, particularly the left-handers, as they curl like snails into their work.

Eloise wrote of learning to drive in the graveyard at midnight in the town of Leominster, Massachusetts. As with a number of my older women students, her father didn't allow her to drive, so she had to sneak out at night, and moonlight was the solution.

Once a month, by the light of the full moon, Eloise met her friend Cynthia on the dirt road that curled among the gravestones. Cynthia had the car—a Model T—and they drove and giggled. Eloise wrote about the chart they kept, listing the moons that allowed them to drive—the harvest moon, the blue moon, the snow moon—and how they almost crashed into the mayor's headstone under a brilliant wolf moon.

Theresa wrote about how all the women's cycles became aligned in the convent, and that she could feel the moods of the sisters shift with the tides. And she wrote, "You could always tell when the older sisters stopped their monthlies because the clean ironed rags lay untouched on the shelf by their beds from then on."

That night when I went home, Jake wanted to call the man in the moon on the telephone.

"I want to call the man in the moon," he demanded, and stomped his four-year-old feet. "How do you call him?" he asked.

He walked into the kitchen, climbed onto the chair by the phone, and picked up the receiver.

"I don't know," I said. "Try 'one, two, three.'"

He carefully dialed those numbers, and of course nothing happened.

"Not home," he said solemnly, then dialed again and repeated his request into the phone.

My back was to him when I heard, "Yes. Are you the man in the moon? Yes? I'm almost five years old," he said. Then he hung up the phone and beamed.

Leaves

As Jake and I were learning how to live our lives without Willem, Sallie suggested we create a Remembering Tree.

"It can be whatever the children want, a drawing they make with things they recall about their loved ones, or it can be a sculpture where they hang things. One child hung his father's driver's license and comb on a tree made out of clay."

Jake and I planted a Texas redbud tree in Riverside Park in honor of Willem. The cemetery fills us with sorrow, so instead we bike down to the tree by the Hudson River in springtime mud and summer heat and autumn leaves and trudge through the snow in winter, and each time we touch the bark with the palms of our hands.

I told Jake that when he's older and mad at me he could go down to the tree alone and talk to his father, to which he just rolled his eyes.

An Address Book

For months after my husband's funeral, on the nights I could not sleep, I rewashed his shirts and stayed up ironing them. I would stand ironing in our "extra" room, which was my husband's study, and also the same room where he died, and I would chant the word *widow* over and over in my head. I had been preparing for it for the fifteen months he was ill, but actually being one was another story.

In the blur of days after his death, visitors turned their heads when passing the extra room. The hospital bed and medical supplies had been returned, but a room where someone has died makes people uneasy.

In some Native American cultures, a marriage stick is given to a couple at their wedding, and notches are later placed for joys and sorrows. Our apartment is our marriage stick, where love was made and doors were slammed. When friends asked if Jake and I were going to move, I was surprised by their question, and they were surprised by my answer. I had no intention of moving. Just because I lost my husband, if I could afford to stay, did I also have to lose my home?

But I know everybody does this widow and widower thing differently. I still carry my husband's grave plot and section number in my address book, in addition to his sleeve and collar size.

After I ironed my husband's shirts I looked at Willem's desk as he'd left it, with the stack of fiftieth-birthday cards and a photo of us eating pizza in the snow on a street corner in Montreal. While Jake slept I put on a quiet waltz on the CD player and danced tiptoe around and around.

As I reclaimed the room, I began to feel more balanced than I ever had before. After you've taken care of someone with cancer, life feels startlingly simple. I feel stronger as a widow than I ever felt when I was single or married.

Kissing

My father's mother lived in Ohio, and on Friday, November 6, 1917, she wrote to the man whom she would marry, my grandfather, whom I never met. I keep the letter in my drawer, with the ink now faded brown, in perfect Palmer penmanship.

Dear Moe,

Yes, you are a honey-boy and you are not too busy to write to me. Honey, haven't we a lot to be thankful for this Thanksgiving? Ah, to think that we have each other! What a pleasant thought. Moe, why do you say I like you, you silly boy, I love you.

Listen dear, it is almost Shabos and I know you would not want me to commit a sin by writing on the Sabbath so I shall close with oceans of love to you.

Your devoted Dora.

There was a tiny smudge of ink on the *d* in "devoted," and she wrote "P.S. Excuse blot. Think of it as a kiss."

My first kiss was in the basement of the Episcopal

church in Bedford, New York, after dancing with Christopher Richter III. "I Know a Little Place by the Side of the Water" was playing on the record player. We kissed as we slow danced. His lips felt like velvet. He was taller, the boys were always taller than I, and I danced on tiptoe with my arms hung around his neck, exposing the little garters from my pantie girdle in those days before panty hose.

Sabina, a student of mine, was the authority on kissing. She had told me to wait four seasons before I married, yet she had been married three times herself. Apparently waiting four seasons was not enough of a test for her.

"The problem is," she wrote, "sometimes you meet someone new and you must kiss them."

I had practiced kissing my hand for six months before I kissed Christopher Richter III, as well as kissing the full-length mirror in my parents' bedroom, until my mother started grilling me about the smudges.

And now, Willem's NY CITY MARATHON T-shirt hangs in Jake's closet, and although it was washed once, it still has something of Willem's smell, which was a mixture of Dutch licorice drops and lemons, and more than once, when I've put Jake's clothes away, I've brushed my lips across that shirt.

A Catalog

The gravestone catalogs do seem to come now in the mail every year along with the Halloween costume catalogs, in eerie regularity, as well as letters requesting that my dead husband join a brain tumor support group. These things usually do not bother me at this point, but at random times I alternate between fits of laughter and still sometimes tears. I don't like it when other people remind me of my loss. I want to be in charge of my grief. I mentioned this to Sallie, and she said, "Look, we'd prefer not to even think about death, but since it happens, to grandparents, to teachers, to people even closer, we have to talk about it, otherwise you make it worse. It's like Port Authority."

"Excuse me?" I said.

"If someone's taking a bus for the first time from sunny California and arriving at Port Authority bus terminal in New York City, it helps to describe the place. It might not be the image of New York City they had in mind. It's not beautiful, but that's the way it is. On the anniversary of your husband's death you'll probably not feel great, but if you look at the calendar and know it's coming, at least you can be prepared. I call that Port Authority."

Telephone

Now that I'm raising a son without his father, I can't stop asking my own father about the subjects I've spent years assigning to my students. Tell me a memory of your first love. Who was your hero when you were a child? What was your biggest fear at night? Did your parents have any superstitions? What was on the walls of your childhood room?

As different as my father and I are, we've always had one secret in common. We're both more comfortable talking to strangers than to people we know very well. I talk to naked women whose names I don't know in the steam room at the health club. At soccer games, standing with the other parents in the wind and rain on the fields by the Hudson River, our gazes steady on our children as they kick their way through childhood, I confess more than anybody wants to hear about my longings and regrets as the seagulls squawk overhead. My father talks to taxi drivers and the guys behind the counter at the delicatessen.

When I was growing up, we always had the easiest conversations when he called from far away, a hotel phone in L.A., a telephone booth in London, or even a conversation from his office in New York City, while I wrapped myself in the phone cord and sat on the kitchen stool.

I consume my father's memories like candy, and for the first time I have the courage to remember my own. Another secret we share is that we love listening to other people's stories.

Dominoes

The day after Willem died, Jake slipped out of bed, solemnly walked into the kitchen, and took the picture of the two of them eating pancakes off the refrigerator. He returned to his room with the picture and slid it under his pillow. Each night for at least a year he would kneel in front of the pillow, lift it, and kiss the picture before he went to bed. Then one day he lifted the pillow to have a pillow fight and said, "It's time to put the picture back on the refrigerator," and he did.

Every few months I get a telephone call that starts with, "A friend's husband just died. She has children. Would you mind talking with her?"

Jake's gotten so used to it he now says, "You talk to the mom. I'll handle the kid."

One widow and child were over on a Saturday evening for dinner. As the mother and I whispered earnestly in the hallway, we overheard the boys talking on the couch in the living room as they watched *Sponge Bob*. They stared at the screen as they spoke.

The other child, Zachary, age five, said, "What did your daddy die of?"

"Brain cancer," said Jake, matter-of-factly. "What about yours?"

"Stomach cancer. Which do you think is worse?" said Zachary.

"Well," said Jake, "you think with your brain, so that kind is bad, but stomach cancer probably hurts a lot. Either way, they're dead. Do you want to play Legos?"

Jake intersperses play and remembering his father all the time.

"Get me a new daddy when I'm at school," he said two weeks after Willem's death. "I need someone to play dominoes with."

Jake plays soccer and baseball and basketball, but if someone wants to throw a football he often declines. As he confided to me, when the other kids weren't around, "Daddy didn't like football."

A Shoebox

Last night my son dragged a chair into his jam-packed closet and climbed up to reach the shoebox where he keeps some of his father's belongings. He brought the shoebox down and placed it on his bed. Then he took out each treasure and smelled it, as if they held special powers. The tiny black tin of Dutch licorice called Potters, the blue and green bow tie Willem wore at our city hall wedding, a phone card from Amsterdam decorated with van Gogh's sunflowers, three stamps from Indonesia. My son held each gem, turning it over, then he took out the clock Willem kept by his side of our bed and solemnly placed it on his bureau, where he already had a clock. I was instructed not to move it.

He does this kind of ritual at different times—when he learned to read three-syllable words, when he learned to Rollerblade—each step forward he reaches back into his early childhood, placing Willem's wristwatch on his small wrist or clomping around in his big slippers.

When a pile of old toys fell down from his closet shelf, I pleaded, "We have to throw away some of your old stuff."

"No," he said firmly, "it reminds me of when I was little."

A Spoon

My son is now ten years old, almost my height, and racing into manhood. One night we were dancing in the kitchen to the Beach Boys while I stirred some carrot and ginger soup. The phone rang and Jake answered it, always eager to make plans with friends.

"No," I heard him say. "No, he's not, he died, but my mom and I are here."

I stood with my wooden spoon poised in the air as if I were going to conduct a symphony, a carved spoon Willem and I had bought at an outdoor market in Lithuania.

It took me a moment to realize he was talking to a telemarketer.

In the springtime of this year something happened. It was a sweet May day and we were riding our bikes down to the baseball fields by the Hudson River. We passed Willem's tree, which was now bursting with tiny plum-colored blossoms.

As we passed by, Jake said softly, "I don't remember him."

"What?" I said, pumping to keep up with his strong legs.

"I don't remember Daddy," he said evenly.

Sallie had said this happens often with kids who lose their parents at a young age. She said there is no predicting when that might be.

I was off balance watching the game. The innings dragged on, Jake was jubilant with his teammates as they pulled into the lead, but I was distracted. I wanted to will him back to remembering his father.

That afternoon, when Jake lay exhausted in his baseball uniform on the couch, I pointed to some photographs in the living room, one of Willem pushing Jake on a tire swing in Central Park, one of the three of us eating raw herring on an Amsterdam street corner, and another of Jake perched on his father's shoulders on the sidewalk outside our building.

Jake didn't make a sound.

Then I put on the audiotape of Willem reading *Curious George* in Dutch.

"No," he sighed. "I don't even remember his voice. Could I have some lemonade please?"

I remember watching an interview with John F. Kennedy Jr., where he said he didn't know if he remembered sitting under his father's desk at the White

House or if seeing all those photographs constructed the memory.

All that effort to remember, I thought, all those talismans in Jake's room. As I poured the lemonade I smiled to myself. I now realized that this was part of it all. Perhaps in fifteen years, or perhaps when he is an old man, Jake will have a memory of his father, perhaps then it will be time to remember again.

AFTERWORD

by Sallie Sanborn, MS
Child Development/Child Life Specialist

I remember Patty's first phone call. In one breath she said, "I got your name from Dr. Lazarus. My husband has brain cancer, and we have a three-year-old boy we adopted from Lithuania. His father is going to die, and I'm not sure what to do or say."

And so we began the work I do, the task of moving toward an understanding of the often nonverbal ways in which children deal with grief and how this fits into the general framework of childhood development. When a parent asks me, "Will my child ever get over this?" my response is that no loss is ever "gotten over" but rather is integrated into the child's life. Grief comes in cycles, on a daily, monthly, and yearly basis. Understanding what the developmental tasks and challenges are for children at different stages of their lives is critical in comprehending how they are perceiving events around them. The experience will redefine itself at every stage of development.

In infancy a baby begins to trust and develop attachment. Although they do not understand death, babies may feel changes in the environment because of changes in the caregiver. The unavailability of parents because of death or illness can cause infants to withdraw and be less responsive, which affects their crying patterns, sleeping, and eating. It is key to provide these babies as much consistent nurturing as possible at this time.

When they are toddlers, children begin to develop autonomy and might understand that a parent is dead, but they will still be confused about it. They might say, "I know Daddy's in Heaven, but he'll be at my birthday party, right?" Gentle repetition of the reality of the situation is helpful. This process can continue until they begin to master the concept cognitively.

Preschoolers understand death as happening to someone else, but they frequently feel they caused the death in some way. When it arises in their play or talk, it is important to regularly remind a child, "Nothing you said or did made Daddy die. His body stopped working because . . ."

School-age children begin to understand the concept of death but are often thinking about it in a different way, with images of ghosts or skeletons. They might begin to appear indifferent about the death, when in reality they are maintaining a close relationship with the image or illusion of the deceased. They might begin to feel shame or guilt about being different from their peers, and they may take comfort with other children who have experienced loss, or they may not. They all find their own comfort, and it is often unspoken comfort.

One of the simplest pieces of advice I give parents is to trust their own instincts when dealing with a child in their care. For children, change is loss. When a child loses a tooth, a shoe, a teddy bear, it's a loss. When a loved one is taken away from the role of being the caregiver either physically or emotionally or both, it is a loss of that parent. In this situation it is important to provide the children with support so that they don't feel as vulnerable.

It's about giving them permission to feel sad. It's appropriate. We don't deny children happy experiences; we have to give them the tools to deal with sad experiences. We have to make an emotional tool bag to help when feelings are scary, sad, and angry, which can be used by parent as well as child.

It's important to explain changes in a child's environment. Tell your children before they hear it from someone else. We know that lack of information is a source of worry for us, and it is for our children as well. They want to know. Tell them about the surgery and medicine that will be used and what the effect could be. Tell them everything the doctors will try to do. They're not afraid of the words *cancer*, *tumor*, and *leukemia*. You can say, "There are a lot of different kinds of cancer. Mommy's cancer is this." Some children don't want to know as much as others, but always answer the questions they ask.

We don't have to be afraid to share difficult information with children. Years ago at Bellevue Hospital in New York City, I was sitting at the bedside of a seriously ill girl who said, "Don't tell my mom I'm going to die." All of us who have worked with ill kids have had that experience, but we're still amazed by it.

As a parent I understand that when you're consumed with your own worry you can't always explain everything to your child right away; it's a gradual process, and I try to respect that process. It's fine for me to sit in my chair and say, "Go tell your child that you have cancer." I know it's not an easy task, but it's always worth doing.

Children feel everything and often feel opposite feelings at once. It's important for them to know it's okay to feel relief when a parent dies after a difficult illness. It's okay to want to be at your dad's funeral but wish you could be at your Little League game. It's okay (and happens frequently at funerals) for a child to ask the surviving parent, "When will you marry again?"

Children want to keep the circle whole. What they say and the questions they ask can be startling, but if you are prepared, you can be an honored witness in keeping their lives together.

RESOURCES

Books for Children

Arnold, Caroline. *What Do We Do When Someone Dies.* New York: Franklin Watts, 1987. (Recommended for ages seven and up.)

Brown, Marc, and Laura Krasny Brown. *When Dinosaurs Die: A Guide to Understanding Death.* New York: Little, Brown and Company, 1998. (Recommended for ages four to nine.)

Buscaglia, Leo. *The Fall of Freddie the Leaf: A Story of Life for All Ages.* Thorofare, N.J.: Charles B. Slack, 1982. (Recommended for all ages.)

Cave, Anne Good. *Balloons for Trevor: Understanding Death.* Saint Louis, Mo.: Concordia Publishing House, 1998. (Recommended for ages four to eight.)

Cohen, Cindy Klein, and John T. Heiney. *Daddy's Promise.* Bloomfield Hills, Mich.: Promise Publications, 1997. (Recommended for ages four to eight.)

Coutant, Helen. *First Snow.* New York: Knopf Publishers, 1974. (Recommended for ages five to eight.)

Douglas, Eileen. *Rachel and the Upside Down Heart.* New York: Dancing Magic Heart Books, 2006. (Recommended for ages four to nine.)

Grollman, Earl. *Straight Talk about Death for Teenagers: How to Cope with Losing Someone You Love.* Boston, Mass.: Beacon Press, 1993. (Recommended for ages thirteen to eighteen.)

Holden, L. Dwight. *Gran-Gran's Best Trick: A Story for Children Who Have Lost Someone They Love*. Washington, D.C.: Magination Press, 1989. (Recommended for ages four to eight.)

Kolf, June Cerza. *Teenagers Talk about Grief.* Grand Rapids, Mich.: Baker Book House, 1990. (Recommended for ages thirteen to eighteen.)

Krementz, Judith. *How It Feels When a Parent Dies*. New York: Knopf, 1988. (Recommended for all ages.)

LeShan, Eda. *When a Parent Is Very Sick*. New York: Little, Brown and Company, 1987. (Recommended for ages nine to twelve.)

Mellonie, Bryan, and Robert Ingpen. *Lifetimes: The Beautiful Way to Explain Death to Children*. New York: Bantam Books, 1983. (Recommended for ages three to nine.)

Munsch, Robert. *Love You Forever*. Willowdale, Calif.: A Firefly Book, 1983. (Recommended for ages three to nine.)

Saltzman, David. *The Jester Has Lost Hist Jingle*. Palos Verdes Estates, Calif.: The Jester Col., Inc., 1995. (Recommended for ages five and up.)

Schultz, Charles. *Why, Charlie Brown, Why?* New York: Topper Books, 1990. (Recommended for ages five to ten.)

Sgouros, Charissa. *A Pillow for My Mom*. Boston: Houghton Mifflin, 1998. (Recommended for ages four to eight.)

Simon, Norma. *The Saddest Time*. Niles, Ill.: Albert Whitman and Company, 1996. (Recommended for ages five to ten.)

Spelman, Cornelia. *After Charlotte's Mom Died*. Niles, Ill.: Albert Whitman and Company, 1996. (Recommended for ages four to eight.)

Varley, Susan. *Badger's Parting Gifts*. New York: Harper-Trophy, 1992. (Recommended for ages four to nine.)

Viorst, Judith. *The Tenth Good Thing about Barney*. New York: Aladdin, 1971. (Recommended for ages five to nine.)

Wolfelt, Alan D. *Healing Your Grieving Heart: 100 Practical Ideas for Kids*. Fort Collins, Colo.: Companion Press, 2001. (Recommended for ages six to twelve.)

———. *How I Feel: A Coloring Book for Grieving Children*. Fort Collins, Colo.: Companion Press, 1999. (Recommended for ages three to eight.)

Zolotow, Charlotte, ed. *Early Sorrow: Ten Stories of Youth*. New York: Harper & Row, 1986. (Recommended for ages thirteen to eighteen.)

Books for Families

Heegaard, Marge. *When Someone Very Special Dies: Children Can Learn to Cope with Grief*. Chapmanville, W.Va.: Woodland Press, 1988.

Jackson, Edgar N. *Telling a Child about Death*. New York: Hawthorn Books, 1965.

McCue, Kathleen. *How to Help Children through a Parent's Serious Illness*. New York: St. Martin's Griffin, 1996.

Nussbaum, Kathy. *Preparing the Children: Information and Ideas for Families Facing Terminal Illness and Death*. N.p.: Gifts of Hope Trust, 1998.

Schaefer, Daniel, and Christine Lyons. *How Do We Tell the Children? A Step-By-Step Guide for Helping Children Cope When Someone Dies*. New York: Newmarket Press, 2002.

Trozzi, Maria. *Talking to Children about Loss*. New York: Perigee, 1999.

Books for Practitioners and Caregivers

Crenshaw, David. *Bereavement: Counseling the Grieving throughout the Life Cycle*. New York: Continuum Books, 1990.

Doka, Kenneth J. *Children Mourning, Mourning Children*. New York: Taylor and Francis Books, 1995.

Jarrett, Claudia Jewett. *Helping Children Cope with Separation and Loss*. Boston: Harvard Common Press, 1982.

Webb, Nancy Boyd. *Helping Bereaved Children: A Handbook for Practitioners*. New York: Guilford Press, 2005.

Wolfelt, Alan D. *Healing the Bereaved Child*. Fort Collins, Colo.: Companion Press, 1996.

Videos

Azimi, Sharene. *Come Feel the Wind*. New York: Cinema Guild, for Bank Street College of Education, 1998.

Ebeling, Carol, and David Ebeling. *When Grief Comes to School*. Bloomington, Ind.: Educational Enterprises, 1991.

Kussman, Leslie. *What Do I Tell My Children?* Sherborn, Mass.: Aquarian Productions, 1992.

Wolfelt, Alan. *A Child's View of Grief*. Fort Collins, Colo.: Center for Loss and Life Transition, 1991.

Web Sites and Organizations

The Center for Loss and Transition
3735 Broken Bow Road
Fort Collins, CO 80506
Phone: 970-226-6050
Web site: www.centerforloss.com

Centering Corporation
A nonprofit bereavement resource center
PO Box 4600
Omaha, NE 68104
Phone: 403-553-1200
Web sites: www.centering.org; www.griefdigest.com

The Dougy Center
A nonprofit center with nationwide
affiliates for grieving children
PO Box 86852
Portland, OR 97286
Phone: 503-775-5683
Web site: www.GrievingChild.org

The Good Grief Program
Provides training, consultation, and crisis intervention
in the area of children's bereavement
1 Boston Medical Center Place, Mat 5
Boston, MA 02118
Phone: 617-414-4005
Web site: www.bmc.org/pediatrics/special/GoodGrief/
overview.html

Making Headway Foundation
A nonprofit organization dedicated to the care, comfort, and
cure of children with brain and spinal cord tumors
115 King Street
Chappaqua, NY 10514
Phone: 914-238-8384
Web site: www.makingheadway.org

Motherless Daughters
Provides assistance and guidance for adult women and young
girls who have lost their mothers
Web site: www.motherlessdaughters.com

Well Spouse Foundation
A national support organization for families and caregivers
of the chronically ill and/or disabled
Web site: www.wellspouse.com

Other Useful Sites

www.childlife.org

www.clgny.com (child life of greater New York)

www.about.com (search: grief and loss; death and dying)

www.comfortzonecamp.org (grief camp)